HOW TO
WRITE A NEWS
ARTICLE

HOW TO WRITE A NEWS ARTICLE

BY MICHAEL KRONENWETTER

A SPEAK OUT, WRITE ON! BOOK
Franklin Watts
A Division of Grolier Publishing
New York / London / Hong Kong / Sydney
Danbury, Connecticut

Photographs copyright ©: Photofest: p. 10; Jay Mallin: pp. 13, 30, 50; Ford Motor Company: p. 17 top; New York Stock Exchange: p. 17 bottom; Gamma-Liaison: pp. 22 (Shock Photography), 76 (Dominique Nabokov); The Miami Herald: p. 28; Wide World Photos: pp. 33, 62, 92; UPI/Bettmann: p. 38; Reuters/Bettmann; p. 67; Rothco Cartoons/Dick Adair, Honolulu Advertiser: p. 95.

Library of Congress Cataloging-in-Publication Data

Kronenwetter, Michael.
How to write a news article / by Michael Kronenwetter.
p.   cm. — (A Speak out, write on! book)
Includes bibliographical references and index.
Summary: Discusses basic aspects of news journalism, including judging what is newsworthy, gathering information, journalistic ethics and bias, and shaping a story.
ISBN 0-531-11238-1 (lib. bdg.) — ISBN 0-531-15786-5 (pbk.)
1. Journalism — Authorship — Juvenile literature. [1. Journalism.]
I. Title. II. Series.
PN4776.K76 1995
808' .06607 — dc20   95-8527
                                                           CIP AC

CONTENTS

HOW TO
WRITE A NEWS
ARTICLE

PART ONE

THE ROLE OF THE NEWS WRITER

Hollywood classics, such as Five Star Final, present some very dramatic, and very unrealistic, images of newspaper offices.

INTRODUCTION

STOP THE PRESSES! STOP THE PRESSES!

It's a classic scene in old movies and television shows.

The cub reporter rushes into the newsroom of the *Big City Star.*

The crowded room is filled with veteran reporters, brimmed hats perched on their heads, sulfurous cigars dangling from their lips. Some are milling about, trading wisecracks. Others are busy picking away at their typewriters with one finger of each hand. Their desks are cluttered with papers, littered with mugs of coffee.

Tearing a page from his typewriter, one of the grizzled old hands snaps his fingers, and an eager young copy boy dashes down the aisle to grasp the sheet and rush it off to the printers. The bustling room is heavy with smoke, and loud with the clatter of the typewriters and the roar of gruff voices.

"Stop the presses!" yells the newcomer, and the noise turns to sudden silence as all eyes turn to him.

The old-timers gape in amazement as the young man runs the length of the crowded room to the door marked "Editor" at the far end.

He bursts through.

Inside his office, the crusty old editor rises from his desk to protest the invasion. But seeing the excitement in the reporter's eye, he stops with his mouth half-open.

"I've got the story!" the young man exclaims. "The mayor's on the take, and I've got the witnesses to prove it. He's resigning in the morning. This is a scoop, boss. Honest. No other paper in town's got it. If we hurry, we can make the morning edition. You've gotta stop the presses. You've just gotta!"

"You bet I will," growls the editor, snatching up the phone on his desk. "Stop the presses!" he orders into it. "We've got a big story coming down."

Hanging up the phone, he crosses to the reporter and gives him a fatherly clap on the back.

"Good work, my boy. I guess you're going to make a real reporter, after all."

The young man beams.

"But getting the story's only part of it," the editor cautions sternly. "Now you've got to write it."

"Yes, sir." Swelling with pride, and eager to get to his typewriter, the young man turns and bolts for the door.

"Write it good," the editor calls him. "But write it fast!"

"Yes, sir!"

* * *

Well, it doesn't quite work that way today. The newsroom of the modern *Big City Star* is no longer filled with clouds of cigar smoke, for one thing. Most newspeople have read too many of their own reports on the hazards of tobacco for them to smoke anymore.

The newsroom is no longer exclusively male, either. It might very well contain as many women as men—if not more. And the editor the young newsperson reports to might be a woman, too.

In today's newsrooms, most people work on word processors, and women and men are more equally represented.

What's more, there is no clatter of manual type-writers. You would be hard pressed even to find an electric typewriter in a newsroom today. Instead, everybody works on word processors, tapping away in near silence, eyes glued to the screen.

Most important, newspaper people don't yell "Stop the presses!" anymore. It's doubtful they ever did.

But, all that aside, the heart of that classic scene still rings true today. There is a real excitement and pride in getting a good story. And whether you're female or male, work on a manual typewriter or a word processor, smoke like a dragster's tire or eat granola bars, your job is still essentially the same. You've still got to get the story, and then you've got to write it well and write it fast.

In this book we will discuss some of what it takes to do just that. The book is intended primarily for student journalists, but it is not about school journalism, as such. Good journalism is good jour-nalism. The basic principles of good reporting are pretty much the same for reporters on student newspapers as they are for major metropolitan dailies. A good story is a good story—and a good editorial is a good editorial—no matter what kind of publication you write it for.

ONE

WHAT'S NEW(S)?

What is the purpose of the news media?

Today our society needs first, a truthful, comprehensive, and intelligent account of the day's events in a context which gives them meaning; second, a forum for the exchange of comment and criticism; third, a means of projecting the opinions and attitudes of the groups in the society to one another; fourth, a method of presenting and clarifying the goals and values of the society; and, fifth, a way of reaching every member of the society by the currents of information, thought, and feeling which the press supplies.[1]

That is how an independent commission defined the job of the news media almost half a century ago, and it still holds true today. Put more simply, the newsperson's job is to inform readers of what's going on in the world around them.

It's a big job, and a big responsibility.

Most people only learn about a small part of the world from their personal experience. They grow up in one or two neighborhoods, in one or two communities. They go to school, get a job, and settle down. During all that time, they have a fairly small, and limited, circle of friends.

They may change jobs, and homes, a few times over the course of their lives. They may even travel a little. But, for the most part, they live their lives within a narrow range. The great majority of the people they share thoughts and experiences with come from the same economic class and social background that they do.

So, where can they learn about the rest of the world? About other places and other people? About the problems those people have, and the things that they do? How does a Kansas wheat farmer learn about life in South Central Los Angeles or in "the projects" of Chicago's Cabrini Green? How does a stockbroker working in downtown Manhattan learn about the plight of laid-off autoworkers in Detroit? How does an African-American teenager in rural Georgia find out about the achievements of black entrepreneurs in the Midwest?

How do any of these people learn what's going in Paris, Baghdad, Tokyo, or Bangladesh?

Yet people need to know about these things. The upsurge in violent crime that first poisoned life in the inner cities has spread even into Kansas. The plight of unemployed autoworkers affects the trading of stocks on Wall Street. The success of black busi-

If autoworkers in Michigan were laid off, how would it affect stockbrokers in New York City? News stories can help people to put things in perspective and prepare for events that may change their life.

nesspeople encourages the hopes and dreams of African-American teens all over the country. Events in distant places affect Americans in all kinds of ways: sometimes dramatically raising or lowering the costs of goods we buy, sometimes leading to wars that claim the lives of many Americans.

Most Americans get vital information about all these things from journalists—from television and radio reporters and, in most detail, from the print journalists who write for newspapers and magazines.

Different journalists explore and explain different parts of their readers' world. Some write about events in a particular community, or even a particular school. Others write about happenings in a particular state or region. Still others deal with foreign lands.

Some are generalists. They write about all sorts of things. Others work specific beats. They write about particular *kinds* of events, such as politics, business, sports, theater, movies, education, medicine, or travel.

But all news writers play the same basic role in their readers' lives. They are sources of information. They are the means by which their readers learn about many of the important events, people, and issues that will affect them.

KINDS OF NEWS

This book is about print journalism, the kind of journalism that appears in newspapers and some magazines. There are five main kinds of print journalism: straight news stories, analysis/background pieces, investigative reporting, human-interest features, and opinion pieces. Each is important, because each plays its own role in fulfilling the purposes of the news media spelled out at the beginning of this chapter.

Straight News

The *straight news story* is the backbone of all journalism. It is the type of story found on the front page, and many other pages, of every newspaper in the world. It is the story that gives basic information about a newsworthy event as directly and as clearly as possible.

The straight news story deals primarily with hard and breaking news—significant events that have just happened, are still happening, or will happen soon. The goal of such a story is to describe the facts and conditions of that event.

When writing straight news, your main concern is making your story accurate and clear. Facts are the whole essence of straight news reporting. Because these stories deal with breaking events, they tend to be written quickly to meet a rapidly approaching deadline. As a result, individual style and writing flair tend to be less emphasized than in other forms of journalism where the writer has more time to rewrite. Nonetheless, straight news reporters should be as concerned about clarity and good composition as any other journalist.

Analysis/Background

Like straight news stories, background pieces are often inspired by breaking news. But, where the straight news story concentrates on describing current events, background pieces try to put those events in perspective. They are designed to help readers understand *why* events are happening, and what those happenings mean.

Other background pieces set out to enlighten the reader about some broad social situation or concern. They may discuss anything from the problem of violent crime in the inner cities to the growing number of the unemployed in once-prosperous suburbs, to the national debt.

Such stories often involve analysis—an attempt to explain the causes, significance, and likely consequences of the reported events. The writer of analysis is giving only an interpretation of why and how things *are*, or how they *might* be in the future. They are often all but indistinguishable from opinion pieces, as the journalist attempts to understand and explain events. The opinion writer is free to go further, and express her or his conviction of how things *ought* to be.

Investigative Reporting
Some news stories take longer and are harder to get than others. For these stories, it is not enough to show up on the scene of some event, ask a few questions, and write your story. You need to investigate.

Investigative pieces can involve all sorts of subjects. They can deal with hard news events or take the form of background/analysis pieces. They can expose the reality behind breaking news, or shed new light on events in the past. But they almost invariably involve information someone is trying to hide, such as a pattern of corruption in some business or government agency, the health hazards of a popular consumer product, or an old, unsolved crime.

To get such stories, you need to dig: to unearth facts buried in old documents, or squirreled away in the memories of people who do not want them to see the light of day. You will need to become a kind of detective, to piece together apparently unrelated information from all kinds of sources, and shape them into a revealing new whole.

Human Interest Features
Unlike straight news stories, which center on events, human-interest features center on people. Perhaps

the most common kind of human-interest story is the profile. A profile is a portrait of a specific individual. The subject of the profile may be a celebrity or it may be someone totally unknown to the general public. Sometimes, it can even be a group: there could be a profile on nuns in a Carmelite convent, for example, or on members of an Olympic bobsled team.

Celebrities, of course, are automatically of interest to many readers, although features about them might focus on their lifestyles or their personal relationships rather than whatever it is that makes them famous. In fact, profiles of celebrities often revolve around elements of their lives that have nothing to do with their fame. Frequently, they focus on things that seem at odds with their celebrity image: a politician's family life, the day-to-day life of a movie star who lives in a small midwestern town, a multimillionaire's passion for dirt-track racing. Such aspects of a public figure's life are used to throw light on his or her "true" character. They serve to make the celebrity more human to readers, more like the readers themselves.

Most human-interest stories, however, don't deal with celebrities at all. They deal with ordinary people. Some of these ordinary people have done extraordinary things, of course—a paper boy who saved his elderly customers from fires, a hairdresser who has the world's largest collection of bobby pins or bubble-gum wrappers. But not always. Sometimes, the whole point of a profile is the ordinariness of its subject. Newspapers frequently run features about typical local citizens, cumulatively presenting an overall portrait of the community. Student papers often run profiles of individual students. Some may be school sports stars, or class officers, but others are not. Picked more or less at random, they represent not the high achiever, but the unexceptional student— the kid other kids can identify with.

Other human-interest features may or may not center around an individual, but they are more concerned with a particular event, place, or human situation than with the person as such. Just about anything can be the subject for a human-interest piece, from life in a small town in the hills of Kentucky to conditions in a big-city nursing home; from the preseason agony of players trying to win a spot on an NFL football team to the joys and disappointments of a Little League baseball season; from the fear of parents waiting for their child to come out of surgery to the tensions backstage on the opening night of a community theater production of *Oklahoma!*

Opinion Pieces

Journalists are usually expected to keep their personal views and feelings out of their reporting, but writers of opinion pieces are encouraged to do just the opposite.

Although they may indicate hard information, their main purpose is just what the name suggests—they express the writer's views on some topic, great or small. The most familiar kind of opinion piece is the editorial that appears in almost every issue of almost every newspaper, but there are several others. They include certain kinds of features, as well as a variety of columns, from political commentary to movie reviews.

Human-interest stories often focus on events that are out of the ordinary. This "canine-interest" item features Jake, a dog who ran for mayor in Erie, Pennsylvania.

Some opinion pieces are written to persuade—that is, to sway readers to the writer's point of view. This is true, for example, of pieces written by partisans who make the case for one side in a political or philosophic debate.

Other opinion pieces are written to provoke action: "Something must be done about this."

Others are intended less to persuade or provoke than simply to bring something to public attention. It may be a person or event the writer believes is particularly noteworthy, someone or something the writer thinks is especially admirable or despicable, or it may be an issue the writer believes to be important. The writer may not even have a firm position on the issue. She or he may simply want to give people something to think about it.

Another kind of opinion piece is intended primarily to promote controversy. Opinion writers like to stimulate arguments. Some of them delight in being deliberately controversial, even inflammatory. Examples of controversy pieces range from "ten best" or "ten worst" lists to columns in which the writer expresses a point of view he or she knows many readers will find outrageous.

Some straight news reporters don't consider opinion writing to be newswriting at all. Yet the two fields often overlap. Many opinion pieces comment on the news, in the form of current political, social, or artistic events. What's more, they frequently contain as much information as other forms of newswriting. These, however, are less concerned with the facts of those events than with their meaning, and with the writer's reaction to them. This makes them fundamentally different from the other forms of journalism that will be discussed.

PART TWO

MINING THE GOLD

TWO

INFORMATION IS GOLD

Fiction writers have one great advantage over news writers—they can make their stories up. Anything they don't know or can't find out, they can imagine. As a reporter, you can't do that. You have to stick to the reality of whatever event you're reporting, or at least to whatever information you can gather about that reality.

For the news writer, information is gold. It is the treasure you must mine and pass along to your readers. This is your stock in trade. Together with whatever talent you possess, it is all you have to work with. But where do you find that gold, and how do you mine it?

At times, you can rely on your own observation. If you have the courtroom beat, for example, you can actually attend the trials you report. You can sit in the courtroom and watch the lawyers and the witnesses, spot their eccentricities and note their mannerisms. You can note what they say. You can study the judge and jury as the trial winds down, and hear their decisions the moment they're announced.

On other beats, however, almost all of your information will have to come from secondhand sources.

Fortunately, there are many of these. Your potential sources of information are limited only by your imagination and energy.

PRINT SOURCES

Published sources provide some of the richest veins of background information. Of course, every journalist should own, or have access to, at least one good dictionary, almanac, atlas, and encyclopedia—as well as at least one style guide—to answer those nagging questions of punctuation and usage that inevitably arise.

It's a good idea to have a library of other guides and directories handy as well, in order to answer the profusion of unpredictable questions that inevitably come up. A typical collection might include an index of local organizations, various *Who's Who*s and professional directories, detailed city and area maps, as well as directories of city, state, county, and federal government agencies.

A local phone book is, of course, an absolute necessity. In addition, you should keep a personal phone book of sources you've used before or might want to use in the future. Along with their addresses and phone numbers, you should make notations of the kind of information they supplied, and whether or not it was reliable. This private record should be jealously guarded, and not just because it is valuable to you as a reporter. It is your duty to preserve the confidentiality of the people listed there.

THE FILES

The best place to look for previously published information about local issues and personalities is often the morgue of your own publication, where past

*Most news publications have "morgues,"
libraries where clippings of past articles
are kept on file for future reference.*

copies are kept. Most newspapers and magazines
keep some kind of library or file of past issues. Many
are indexed. Some even have individual articles
clipped and arranged by subject matter. These "clip
files" are invaluable for learning what your col-
leagues and predecessors have already discovered
about almost everything imaginable.

Published indexes of several major newspapers—including the *New York Times* and the *Wall*

Street Journal—can be checked for relevant articles on national and international issues. These indexes, as well as microfiched or otherwise reproduced copies of the papers themselves, are available for reference at many libraries.

Relevant articles in magazines and other publications can be located using regularly updated indexes, such as *The Reader's Guide to Periodical Literature*, which are also available at most libraries.

DOCUMENTS

A plethora of records and documents are readily available from virtually every level and branch of government. The birth and death records of virtually every citizen, the financial balance sheets of every public stock company, and the names and address of every public official are just some of the many pieces of information easily accessible to anyone who knows where to look.

The complete texts of all U.S. Supreme Court decisions since the country was founded are available in printed form in many libraries, along with the decisions of your state supreme court. What's more, periodical federal and state registers contain the details of every current state and government regulation.

NONPRINT SOURCES

These days, much of the same information available in print—and much that is not yet available in that form—can be found in cyberspace. Computers have become valuable keys for unlocking the stores of information contained in those electronic treasure boxes known as databases. Depending on your computer resources, you can discover an incredible variety of facts just by punching in the right codes on your PC.

Databases are made available to subscribers through services known as data banks. Some of these data banks contain detailed indexes of information available from a variety of sources; others provide summaries, or abstracts, of articles, reports, and other publications; still others provide whole articles, documents, or even books that you can call up on your computer screen. Try to get your publication to get hooked into the appropriate data banks. If not, you may have more luck at your public library.

The recent libraries of more than 100 different

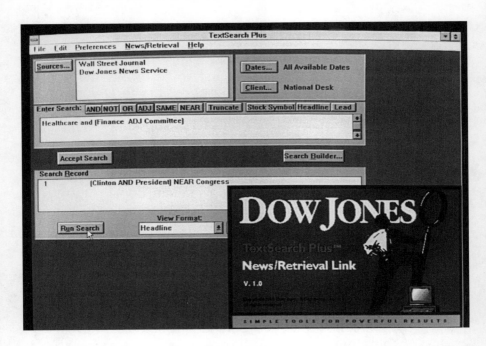

On-line databases can be invaluable reference sources, offering quick access to information on a wide variety of topics.

newspapers can be accessed through the *DataTimes* and *Vu/Text Information Services*, for example.[1] The *Wall Street Journal* is available from the Dow Jones News Retrieval, and still more financial information can be found in the *Standard and Poor's News* data bank. *Nexis* offers the texts of articles from a variety of magazines and periodicals, while *Newsearch* provides a detailed index of recent articles in almost 1,500 different periodicals. In addition, the Library of Congress provides an excellent database of government and other publications.

Depending on your beat, you might find any one of hundreds of specific data banks useful. Want a demographic statistic? *The American Statistics Index*, compiled by the Congressional Information Service, will tell you where to find it. Want information about doings in Congress, but don't have time to thumb through the entire *Congressional Record*? Indexed summations of the *Record*, updated weekly, are available from the *Congressional Record Abstracts* data bank.

HUMAN SOURCES

Newspapers, books, magazines, documents, and data banks can provide you with lots of valuable information, but they are no substitute for the richest of all veins of information: human beings.

No published source can tell you about an event as quickly as an eyewitness can, and no published source can give you the feel of that event like someone who was actually there. No data bank can help you grasp the reality of life in your community the way talking to the people who live there can. A book might be able to tell you everything you need to know about some esoteric subject you have to explain to your readers, but it can't answer your questions. You can't check with it to make sure you really understand what you're being told.

As a newswriter, you will need to meet all kinds of people, from the famous to the obscure, as both sources and subjects of your work. This introduction to a vast variety of people is one of the greatest benefits of the journalistic profession, and sometimes one of its greatest drawbacks as well. Some of the people you meet will be charming, bright, and inspiring, and so interesting that you will have to tear yourself away. But others will be downright boring, boorish, and annoying—and some may be dangerous.

The kinds of people you will need as sources will vary from story to story. If you're doing a feature on the accomplishments of the winner of the Nobel Prize for Economics, you will want to talk to people who understand that "dismal science," and, if possible, to the Nobel laureate. If on the other hand you're reporting on your city's homeless population, you will want to talk to people living on the streets.

You may need only one source for a particular story, or you may need many. If you're doing a brief item on a minor accident, a brief chat with the policeman who went to the scene will probably be enough. If you're doing a major investigative report on toxic leaks from a local chemical factory, you will want to speak to all sorts of people: officials and workers of the company; representatives of government agencies whose job is to regulate hazardous wastes; independent chemical engineers who can fill you in on the science involved; residents of the neighborhood where the factory is located, who might be in danger from the leaks; public-health doctors who can explain the potential threat to them.

Some sources you will need only once. If you interview residents of an isolated farm community for a tornado story, you will probably never need to talk

People may be the best source of information
a journalist can use when composing a news
article. It is important that news writers give
eyewitness accounts accurately and state
only what has been given on the record.

to those people again. If, on the other hand, you have a regular beat, you will want sources you can come back to over and over again. In fact, one of your main tasks as a beat reporter will be to find and cultivate regular sources, people who can be counted on to give you reliable information on an ongoing basis. If you're on the crime beat, you'll want to get to know a lot of cops, and maybe some criminals as well. If your beat is business, you'll want to get on a familiar basis with local business and union officials. If you're a sports reporter, you'll need to get to know as many athletes as possible.

TALKING ON AND OFF THE RECORD

Much of the value of your relationship with a source depends on mutual trust. You need to know that you can rely on what the source tells you, and the source needs to know that you can be relied on not to betray their confidence.

Betray their confidence? What confidence can you be expected to keep? You're a reporter, after all. Your job is to publish information, not keep it secret. Why would you even want information, except to share it with your readers?

In the reporter's ideal world, things would be as simple as that. But the real world is not that simple, and sources are not always that open. The reality is that many people are reluctant to share what they know with you, and will do so only under certain conditions. Sometimes, those conditions involve a promise to keep some or all of the information secret (including the source's identity) in return for other information you are free to publish.

This is an uncomfortable situation for you as a reporter. As a reporter, your first responsibility is to your readers, and it goes against the ethical grain to agree to keep any information from them. On the other hand, you may not be able to get the particular information this source can give you in any other way.

Over the years, journalists and sources have resolved this problem by establishing a number of different understandings—conditions under which reporters will sometimes agree to receive information.

The first, best, and most common way for a reporter to receive information from a source is *on the record*. This means that anything the source tells you is fair game, and can be used in any way you see fit.

Sometimes, however, a source won't talk unless the reporter agrees not to use his or her name. Reporters are reluctant to agree to this because the identity of the source is often an important piece of information in itself. But some sources have good reason to want to keep their identities secret. This is true, for example, of so-called whistle-blowers, government workers, or other employees who have information that will reflect badly on their bosses. It may also be true of people whose information involves criminal activities, which they either witnessed or participated in themselves. These sources may have a legitimate fear of reprisals—the loss of a job, a term in jail, or even physical violence—if their identities become known.

In such cases, the reporter may agree to take the information *on background*. This means, in effect, that the information will be used, but the name of the source will be kept hidden. Background is frequently used by political reporters, who develop regular sources among government workers and political activists. Reporters will frequently try to describe a background source as best they can without revealing his or her actual identity. Terms such as "a female employee," or a "high-ranking campaign official" are used to give readers some idea of the position—and therefore, the credibility—of the source.

By far the least desirable condition under which a reporter can accept information is *on deep background* or *off the record*. This means that the reporter agrees not to use the information at all. At first blush, deep background seems pointless. Why would any sane source tell a reporter something the reporter would never use? And why would any reporter ever agree to receive it under those conditions?

Sources may want to give information off the record for any one of several reasons. The most obvious is to keep you from using it. Once you have taken information on deep background, you are ethically bound not to reveal it. This is, of course, a very good reason to be wary of ever agreeing to speak to anyone off the record.

There are, however, some situations in which deep background may serve both your source's interest and your interest as a reporter.

Say the police chief of your community has a daughter who is rumored to be involved with illegal drugs. If true, that would be a legitimate news story. Now imagine that you have discovered that the daughter has checked into an institution famous for treating drug and alcohol addictions. This might well be evidence that the rumor is true, and your paper may be inclined to publish the story. Speaking off the record, however, the police chief might be willing to explain that her daughter is not being treated for drugs but for unrelated emotional problems. In this case, deep background would serve the chief's interests by protecting the daughter's privacy. It would serve your interests as well, by preventing you from publishing an accurate but misleading story.

Another reason sources might want to speak on

deep background is to defend their own actions and prevent unjust criticism. A district attorney coming under fire for ending the prosecution of a mob killing for no apparent reason might explain, off the record, that she has dropped that case to prevent the exposure of undercover police officers who have infiltrated the mob and are working to expose even more serious crimes. For obvious reasons, she would not want this explanation published. By speaking off the record, however, she would hope to avoid further press criticism.

In the above cases, good arguments can be made that responsible reporters should take the information off the record, and agree not to publish what they know. But such circumstances are rare.

What's more, some journalists believe that deep background is never acceptable, even in situations like these. They emphasize that the function of journalists is to provide information to the public. The press, they insist, is nothing more than a conduit. What is important is not what the journalist knows, but what the public knows. Therefore, they believe, a journalist must never agree to withhold information from the public for any reason whatsoever.

Most modern journalists would not go that far. They accept the argument that getting some information off the record is sometimes better than not getting it at all. One thing most journalists would agree on, however, is that the ultimate object of any deal should be to get good, accurate information to their readers. While some might agree not to share all the information they acquire, they must never agree to distort the information they do publish.

YOUR RELATIONSHIP WITH SOURCES

As a beat reporter, you need to get to know your regular sources, and let them know you. Whenever pos-

When Washington Post *reporters Bob Woodward and Carl Bernstein investigated the Watergate scandal, much of their information was accepted on deep background.*

sible, establish on-going, friendly relationships with them. "Friendly," however, does not mean becoming actual friends. On the contrary, you need to be careful about getting too close to your sources. Friends expect favors.

Despite your best efforts, a friendship with a source may occasionally develop. This is not a disaster. But it does make for problems. Your first loyalty in your relationship with a source should be to your job as a reporter. That relationship is a business relationship, and both you and your source should understand that fact.

Whether your source is an old acquaintance or a stranger, you need to understand that your relationship is a two-way street. What you, as a reporter, want from the source is obvious. But what the source wants from you is often less clear.

Sources share information for several reasons. Some simply enjoy being in a position to tell what they know. Others hope to be quoted in your story and see their names in print. But others have something to gain. Just as you use your source as means of acquiring information, your source may be using you to get that information out. People involved in politics will be eager to give you information that reflects well on politicians they support, or badly on those they oppose. Business sources may want the public to know about good things their company is doing, or may want to put the best light possible on business setbacks.

You must try to recognize the self-interest of your source, and how that self-interest might affect the reliability of what she or he tells you. Always be cautious about taking at face value what a self-interested source tells you. Many sources will fudge the truth, or even lie, to gain an advantage. Others will tell you part of the truth—the part that benefits them—but hide the rest. Sources may even mislead you inadvertently. Personal prejudice or self-interest may fog their vision and keep them from seeing the truth clearly themselves.

The fact that someone has an obvious bias, or even a financial interest in a story, doesn't mean that what they tell you is false. Some sources make it a point to be extremely precise when talking to the press, even when their own interests are involved. Even strong advocates of a cause may strive to be honest and accurate when making their case. Many people, after all, are naturally honest. Others realize that telling the truth is in their own best interest in the long run. If they want to establish a trusting relationship with you, a relationship that can be helpful to them in the future, the information they give you has to be reliable.

By the same token, the fact that someone has no obvious bias doesn't mean that they're telling the truth. They may have a bias, or interest, you're not aware of; they may simply be poor observers; or they may have unreliable memories.

The reality is that people don't always know what they know and what they don't know. As a student, haven't you ever been sure you had the right answer to a test question, but found out that it was wrong when the test was corrected? Or haven't you been sure that something had happened on Wednesday, only to find out that it was on Tuesday after all? Most people have. And your sources will be the same way. Sometimes, they will tell you things as honestly and completely as they can—and still be absolutely wrong.

THE TWO-SOURCE "RULE"

The fact that someone tells you something doesn't make it true. The fact that a piece of information appears in a book or newspaper—or shows up in a data bank—doesn't make it true, either. You should double check your information whenever possible.

Ideally, any potentially controversial fact—and particularly any information that would reflect badly on some individual or organization—should be supported by at least two independent sources. "Independent" means that neither can depend on the other for its own information. If Mr. Tellall gives you the information, you cannot verify his claim by checking with Mrs. Bigears, who got the very same information from the very same Mr. Tellall.

In the past, responsible news organizations insisted on this so-called two-source rule. Today, many are willing to make exceptions to it. Whether your editors insist on it or not, it's a good idea to apply this rule to your own reporting. If you do not, you'd better be sure that your single source is an extremely reliable one.

But how do you do that? How can you tell if a source, human or otherwise, is reliable? The two-source rule helps, but there is no magic test. The best evidence, of course, is experience. If you have used the same source in the past, and the information has checked out, chances are good that it will check out again. But even experience is no guarantee.

Whenever something a source tells you seems odd or unlikely, check it out. If something sounds wrong to you, it probably is. If you can't find a second, independent source for the information itself, you have two other possibilities, depending on the nature of the information. If your source is an expert who has given you suspicious facts or a controversial opinion in his field, find another expert in the same field. Your second expert may not be able to verify, or debunk, the information itself, but he or she may be able to advise you about the *likelihood* or *reasonableness* of what your source has told you.

If you can't find proof or disproof of the information, you may be able to check out the reliability of your source as a source. Find people who can tell you about the person's reputation for accuracy and truth telling, or lack of it.

There will be many times when what you learn will be inconclusive. You won't feel sure about the information. It could well be true, but it could also be false. In that case, you must use your journalistic judgment to decide whether or not to use the information and, if you do, whether or not to caution your reader about the credibility of the information.

Always remember, whatever your sources—print, nonprint, or human—your source's credibility becomes your credibility. If your source is wrong, your story will be wrong, too.

THREE

INTERVIEWING

Whether you're questioning an eyewitness to a violent crime, exploring the emotions of the quarterback who just threw the winning pass in the homecoming game, or sitting down for an in-depth conversation with a famous scientist, asking questions is an important part of your job as a journalist.

MAKING CONTACT

There are many ways to get in touch with people you want to interview, from writing them a letter or calling them on the phone, to appearing at their door or walking up to them on the street.

Which approach to take depends on the kind of interview you're seeking. If you're on the scene of an event, such as an accident or a political speech, and you want information about what's occurred, you'll need to approach people directly and immediately. If you're dealing with other breaking news, and you're on a deadline, speed is still at a premium and you'll probably want to reach people by phone. If what you want is an in-depth interview with a public figure, on the other hand, you will need to approach them in advance, in order to make a more formal appointment.

But can you just approach a perfect stranger—and perhaps even a prominent stranger at that—and ask to talk? Sure you can. Like a salesperson, a journalist has to have the confidence—or the gall—to press questions on perfect strangers.

Some young reporters feel uncomfortable about doing this. And why shouldn't they? Many people are reluctant to talk to reporters. Some are actively hostile. No one likes to be rejected, much less to be verbally abused. And a reporter faces these prospects every time she or he approaches a potential source. But rejection does not occur as often as novice reporters fear.

Depending on your beat, most people will be at least as friendly and polite as the reporter who approaches them. Lots of people, in fact, will be eager to talk to you. It makes some feel important that a reporter wants to hear what they have to say. Others have information they want to share. Still others have a desire to please, and feel an obligation to talk to anyone who wants to talk to them.

Nonetheless, it is true that some people will not want to talk to you. That is their right. No one is required to talk to the press. As a reporter, you have the right to ask. As individuals, they have the right to refuse.

TIPS FOR CONDUCTING INTERVIEWS

Being a good interviewer involves several different skills.

You must be able to ask the right questions, to coax answers out of people who may not want to give them, and to stem the flow of words from subjects who want to talk too much. Perhaps most important of all, you must be able to pick the nuggets of accurate and valuable information out of the mountains of misleading and useless answers you may receive. Each of these skills is developed primarily through practice. There are, however, some things you can do right now to make your interviews more productive.

DO RESEARCH • The better the preparation, the better the interview is likely to be. The first step in preparing for an interview is research. You need to find out as much as possible about the person you're going to talk to, and about the subject you're going to cover.

If you're going to interview a famous baseball player, you'd better know what position he plays, what his past achievements have been, and how his current season is going. If you don't, he's going to recognize your ignorance very quickly, and give you unresponsive answers, if he bothers talking to you at all.

If you're going to interview a member of the local school board about a controversial policy, you should find out everything you can about the issue, including your subject's position on the question. Only then will you be able to ask intelligent questions, the kind that will prompt interesting and enlightening answers.

Above all, don't try to bluff. If, for some reason, you absolutely can't do any research in advance and end up interviewing someone cold, on a subject you know nothing about, you're in real trouble. The best thing you can do is confess your ignorance at the top of the interview, throw yourself on the interviewee's mercy, and hope he or she has a kind heart.

PREPARE YOURSELF • Once you've done the necessary background research, spend some time thinking about the interview itself. Now that you know something about the person you'll be talking to, what approach are you going to use to get your subject to talk? Are you going to try to put the interviewee at ease, or are you going to be confrontational? (The first of those alternatives is almost always better.)

Most important, you need to decide what the purpose of the interview will be. What do you want to learn? Then you must think about the kinds of questions you will have to ask to elicit that information.

Some reporters like to prepare a list of specific questions they want to ask, along with possible follow-ups. Others simply note down a few important points they want to be sure to cover. Even if you have a detailed list, however, ask them as naturally as possible. Obviously reading off a catalog of prepared questions will introduce a stiffness and formality that interferes with good communication.

When preparing, try not to design questions that can be answered yes or no. You want to encourage the subject of your interview to talk openly: to give you information—and quotes—not monosyllables.

In any case, you will need to remain flexible during the interview itself, ready to explore unexpected paths of information that may open up. Be careful, however, not to let yourself be so distracted by interesting byways that you neglect to get the information you came for. Ideally, the more you know about the subject of the interview, and about what you want to find out, the more able you should be to follow the interview wherever it may lead.

BE EARLY • If you have an appointment, be early. You may end up waiting a little longer, but you might also be able to begin early, and that could mean more time for your interview. Above all, don't be late. There's no sense in irritating your subject before you even get started. You want him or her to be in as friendly, talkative, and responsive a mood as possible. Besides, if the interview is late in getting started, you may not have enough time to find out everything you want to know.

BE FRIENDLY • A lot of people are wary and suspicious of the press. Being friendly can disarm potential hostility and put interviewees at their ease. Has your research revealed anything you and your interviewee have in common? Someone you both know? A shared interest in the local sports team? If so, you might bring it up, briefly, as a way of breaking the ice. But . . .

BE BUSINESSLIKE • Don't take too long on introductions. Get to the point promptly and ask your questions clearly, concisely, and directly. If the subject is not used to being interviewed, she or he will take comfort in your professionalism. If the subject is a veteran, he or she will appreciate it even more.

REMEMBER WHO'S THE INTERVIEWER AND WHO'S THE INTERVIEWEE • You're probably a fascinating person with lots of interesting things to say. But when you're interviewing someone else, it is not the time to say them. Some interviewees are naturally interested in other people, even journalists who are interviewing them. They may want to spend the interview drawing you out, instead of being drawn out themselves. Remember that you're there to find out what they know, not to share your insights, however brilliant those might be.

DON'T BE TOO NICE. (BUT DON'T BE MEAN, EITHER.) • When you have a hard question to ask, ask it. You may find yourself liking the people you interview, even feeling sorry for them, but you mustn't shy away from areas they find embarrassing or difficult. Those are often the very areas you are there to explore. On the other hand, don't go out of your way to be antagonistic or combative. There is no need to prove how tough you are, and being offensive may make the subject less willing to talk. Just ask the questions that you need to ask to find out what your readers need to know.

CHECK ANSWERS • When you are not sure that the person you're interviewing is telling you the truth, ask for evidence. Depending on the nature of the question, that evidence might be in the form of documentation, or it might be the names of other people who can verify what you're being told. Once again, there is no need to be confrontational. If the information you're being given is in any way controversial, most subjects will understand your desire for confirmation. And always remember that, even if the information is wrong, the subject may not be deliberately lying to you. He or she may just be mistaken.

LISTEN TO WHAT THE SUBJECT IS ACTUALLY SAYING, NOT JUST TO THE WORDS • The single most important thing to do when interviewing anyone is to listen carefully. This seems obvious, but too many interviewers hear the subject's words, and even memorize many of them, without trying to understand what the person is really means. You must develop the ability to grasp not just what the subject is saying, but what he or she is trying to express. When you suspect that the two may not exactly match, ask clarifying questions.

RECORDING THE INTERVIEW

Unless you're blessed (or cursed) with a foolproof memory, you should always have some way of recording what your subject says. If you're a good note taker, a notebook and a pencil or pen will do fine. Be sure to have an extra one handy, however, in case the pen runs dry or the lead breaks. The rhythm of a good interview can be destroyed by the need to sharpen a pencil, or to search for a new pen.

Many reporters—including some who take exhaustive notes—like to use a micro-recorder, or some other recording device, to make an exact copy of what is said in the interview. It helps to avoid careless mistakes.

If you do plan to record the interview, it's a good idea to ask subjects if they mind. If they say they do, you can explain that a recording will serve as a protection for them as well as for you. If they still object, however, it's probably a good idea to put the recorder away and rely on notes. The important thing in any interview is to get the subject to talk as freely and completely as possible. If a recorder interferes with that process, then get rid of it.

If you are thinking of using a recorder, make sure that the machine is working before you set out for the interview, and that the batteries are fresh. Even if they are, take extras along, in case the one in the machine run down.

If the interview could be a long one, you'll need to bring extra tapes as well. Be aware of how long the tape runs on a side, so you can turn or change the tape promptly and not miss anything. It's a good idea to check the recorder every so often during the course of the interview, just in case there's some kind of malfunction.

Even when taping their interviews, many journalists like to keep notes as well. The note-taking process itself can help keep you focused during the interview process, by keeping track of the most important elements, and potential quotes, as you go along.

Most often, you will probably not have the time to go through the entire tape when the time comes to work on your piece. Instead, you will usually want to cull the tape for specific points or quotes. The more detailed your notes, the easier it will be to find those spots on the tape later.

Just as you need to bring the proper equipment to tape-record your interview, you need the proper equipment to take notes. This may seem obvious, but it's sometimes so obvious that reporters forget to check that they have everything before they set out. A pen and notebook is not enough. Always bring an extra pen, in case the ink runs out in the first one. And a couple of pencils, in case it rains and you need to take notes outside. And a pocket pencil sharpener. And be sure to check that there's still room in your notebook.

Some journalists prefer not to take notes at all, however. Instead, they record their interviews and transcribe the tapes later. They feel that it is easier to talk to the subject—to make eye contact, and to observe them—without having to fiddle around with a pencil and notepad at the same time. Whatever your preference, the important thing is to have some reliable record of what has been said.

When interviewing subjects, journalists should come prepared with pens or pencils and a notepad.

FOUR

ATTRIBUTIONS

Information is the heart and soul of any news story, and all information comes from somewhere. We have already discussed what some of those sources might be. But how relevant is the source when it comes to actually using the information in your story? Should you identify the source within the story itself? If so, how should you identify it?

WHY ATTRIBUTE?

Much of the information in a typical news story can simply be stated as a fact. "A storm swept through the city yesterday . . ." "The Republicans have a solid majority in the state legislature . . ." But other information needs attribution. That is, you have to say where you got it.

Why do you need to attribute information at all? There are several reasons. One is to give credit. Certain kinds of information "belong" to someone else, and it is customary—and legally necessary, in some cases—to acknowledge that ownership. This is true, for example, for information collected and published by other reporters, as well as for certain kinds of quotes.

There are other reasons as well. Attribution can lend authority to your information. Identifying your source is particularly helpful when it comes to any information that might raise the question in the reader's mind: "How does the reporter know that?"

Still another reason for attributing information is to help the reader judge its credibility. If there is any question about the reliability of the source, the reader has a right to know it. What's more, you and your publication are taking sole responsibility for the accuracy of any information that is presented without a source.

WHEN TO ATTRIBUTE

How do you decide which information to attribute? One general principle is that information which is self-evident and indisputable does not need attribution, while you should give a source for any information that might be open to question.

More specifically, you need to *identify the source of:*

• Anything quoted or reprinted from a published source. This is sometimes not just a matter of journalistic ethics, but a legal requirement. You must give credit to the original author of any quote you use in your article. This may be true of certain material you paraphrase as well.
• Direct quotes of all kinds, whether from public documents, speeches, interviews, or any other source. A direct quote means the use of someone's exact words. Virtually anything you put inside quotation marks should be attributed.
• Any information whose source has a real bearing on its credibility. This is particularly true of information provided by people or organizations with an ax to grind. If a spokesperson for a politi-

cian gives you favorable information about her, that is one thing. If her opponent gives you information that reflects poorly on her, that is another thing. You should be wary of both kinds of information, and try to verify them from other, more objective sources. If you cannot, but still choose to use the information, you need to let the readers know where it came from.

• Charges, accusations, and criticism against individuals. In general, you should give a source for any information whose publication will cast someone else in a bad light. As we shall see in the chapter on ethical standards, this kind of potentially damaging information is dangerous stuff, and should be used with care. Its source is always relevant.

• Any information received over the telephone or by fax.

• Speculation. Guesses and predictions are not appropriate to most stories. Still, some stories require conjecture about the possible causes of current events, or what is likely to happen in the future. You should clearly label such information as the speculation it is, and identify its source.

On the other hand, you *do not* need to give a source for:

• Firsthand information. As a reporter, it is your job to observe and report what you have seen. You do not need to name other sources for what you have seen yourself.

• Matters of public record. Government statistics and reports, court records, and so on, belong to the public and can be used without concern. In such cases, you may want to identify the source (to lend authority, for example), but you don't have to do so.

• Common knowledge. You do not have to name a source for facts that are well known and non-controversial. This includes historical information. *The Marshall Plan helped Europe rebuild after World War II. . . . Richard Nixon resigned from the presidency because of the Watergate scandal.* It also includes general knowledge about current events, such as the fact that there is a high level of illegitimate births among young American women and a widespread fear of violent crime in the nation's cities. (If you choose to quantify such general information, however—"26 percent of births are to unmarried women," or "60 percent of American city-dwellers fear to walk the streets at night"—you should give the source of the figures.)

• Any information already available from a large number of sources. It would be silly, as well as unnecessary, to name a specific source for information that is available in any encyclopedia, or that has recently been front-page news in every paper in the country.

QUOTES

There are different kinds of quotes. The first and most obvious is the direct quote, in which the actual words of the speaker (or document) are used and enclosed within quotation marks. Such quotes should be scrupulously accurate. Anything less would be unfair to the person quoted, as well as potentially misleading to the reader. The only widely recognized exception to the accuracy rule allows small changes to clear up confusing or incorrect grammar.

Direct quotes should also be as complete as possible. Words may sometimes have to be left out for reasons of length or clarity, but where words of any significance are omitted, the gap should be indicated with ellipsis points (. . .).

Other quotes can be paraphrased, putting the person's thoughts in different words, often to make the point more clear or succinct. Paraphrased quotes are not put in quotation marks, since they do not use the actual words of the original speaker or writer. When using this kind of quote, you must be careful not to distort the source's meaning.

Attribution of quotes is especially important. This is because a quote is a special kind of information. It has two separate prongs. The first prong is the quote itself: that is, the fact that the source said what it is that is being quoted. The second prong is whatever information is conveyed within the words of the quote itself. This distinction is important because the fact that the first prong may be true does not mean that the second is true as well. In other words, the quoted statement might be the truth or it might be a lie.

FORM

Most attributions follow the same simple pattern: noun and verb. "Mr. Whoever said . . . ", "Ms. Whosis declared . . . ", etc.

"President Clinton announced" or "Pope John Paul II proclaimed" is enough of an attribution for any quote. But "Joe Obscure said" is practically meaningless. Who is Joe Obscure? What does he know, anyway? Why should the reader care what he says? In such cases, you need to provide the reader with identifying information: "union official Joe Obscure," or "Joe Obscure, an expert in international development working for the United Nations."

The same principle applies when the quoted source is an organization instead of an individual. "The Ku Klux Klan" is probably enough of an attribution for most readers. However, "the Christian

Patriots" is not. For that group, some explanation, such as "a small but strongly anti-Semitic white supremacist group" is necessary.

Identification may also be required when the source of a quote or other information is a public document, a published report, or a study. Ordinarily, such an attribution needs to be brief. This doesn't mean that it can be written carelessly, or with little thought, however. Questions you might need to consider when deciding how much attribution to give include the following:

Did some group or organization commission the report? Do they have an ax to grind? Who actually conducted the study, or wrote the report? What is their reputation? Are they considered reliable?

As with individuals, whenever the author or sponsor of a report has an obvious bias, some indication of that bias should be given in the attribution: "a Democratic think tank;" "a pro-life group;" "a study commissioned by the Republican National Committee," etc.

WHAT'S IN A NAME?

Whenever you identify a source, you should do so as objectively as possible. This is not always as easy as it might seem.

Take the term "Democrat Party," for example, when applied to the older of the two major political parties in the United States. "Democrat Party" may seem to be nothing more than a shorter form of "Democratic Party," but it is actually a term coined by Republicans to imply that the Democratic Party is not really democratic at all, or at least, no more democratic than any other party.

Many Republicans use "Democrat Party," but no Democrats do. Democrats insist on calling their organization "the Democratic Party," the name by which it was universally known for over a century. Using "Democrat Party" enlists you, however unintentionally, on the side of the Republicans, taking a mild swipe at the Democrats.

Activists who believe that women should keep their right to get abortions call their movement "pro-choice." Activists who disagree with them on the issue call them "pro-abortion." By the same token, those who believe that abortion is wrong call themselves "pro-life." Those who disagree call them "anti-abortion" or "anti-choice."

Short of getting inside their heads, there's no way to tell why individual journalists choose one term or another when writing about these groups. It seems, however, that a bias, conscious or otherwise, often creeps in. Liberal journalists tend to use "pro-choice" and "anti-abortion" more than conservative journalists, who usually use the other terms.

Many people and organizations complain about the labels that careless journalists stick on them, and they are often right to protest. The press in general needs to be more sensitive to the nuances of the terms we use to describe both people and organizations.

In general, it is best to call a person or group whatever it chooses to call itself. The decision then becomes, in a sense, a simple matter of fact. After all, an organization has a right to its own name, just as people do. John Smith is John Smith. You may consider "John" a fine name, and John Smith a terrible person, but he is still John Smith. As a reporter, you have no right to decide that "John" is too good a name for him, and call him "Jack" Smith instead.

If you feel a journalistic obligation to warn readers that a group's name is misleading, you should do so directly, not by the childish tactic of refusing to call them by their chosen name.

PART
THREE

THE RESPONSIBILITIES
OF A NEWS WRITER

FIVE

ℰTHICAL STANDARDS

Journalism is a privileged profession in the United States, and journalists are privileged people. The press, which includes all the news media, is given a special protection by the First Amendment to the Constitution of the United States, which states that "Congress shall make no law abridging the freedom . . . of the press."

As a practical matter, this means that there are very few outside checks on how journalists do their jobs. The First Amendment forbids the government from taking action against the press. The Supreme Court has made certain, very limited, exceptions to that rule, but most of those exceptions involve national security or gross indecencies. They have very little effect on the way most newspeople do their jobs. Even private individuals find it almost impossible to win a lawsuit against a journalist, no matter how irresponsible or unfair that journalist has been.

Because journalists are not much policed or regulated from outside their profession, they must be especially careful to police themselves. Along with their special privileges and protections comes an additional responsibility. That is the duty to carry out their work according to the ethics—the professional and moral standards—of good journalism.

But what are the ethics of good journalism? That is not always clear. Journalists in different media—newspapers, television, magazines, and radio—tend to follow somewhat different ethical rules. Even within a single medium, there is often disagreement over what is, and what is not, ethical. As Katherine Graham, the publisher of the *Washington Post*, has said, there is no unifying set of ethical standards in journalism today. "But there are standards."[1]

Because no outside force has the authority to impose ethical standards on the press, journalists must set their own standards. Many newspapers and other news organizations have written ethical guidelines for themselves. Not all agree on details. Each is adopted to the specific needs and circumstances of the news organization involved. Some organizations, for example, will pay for news tips, or even pay prominent people for interviews, while others refuse.

In addition, individual journalists often have their own standards of what they will and will not do, which go beyond those of their news organization. Some publications, for example, will allow theater critics to accept free tickets to shows they plan to review, but some critics prefer to pay their own way. They don't want to feel indebted in any way to a production they may feel deserves a bad review.

As a journalist, you have to make all kinds of judgments in the course of writing a story. *Should I include this fact or not? Is this adjective too strong? Is this source reliable? Is this fact really relevant to the story?* Ethical concerns are often central to these journalistic decisions. Too often, unfortunately, they get lost in the jumble of other factors, or forgotten in the race to meet a deadline.

Ultimately, you have to make each judgment on a

In January 1995, CBS was criticized for violating journalism ethics when it broadcast Kathleen Gingrich's confidential statement to Connie Chung about comments her son, Speaker of the House Newt Gingrich, had made regarding First Lady Hillary Rodham Clinton.

case-by-case basis. Each set of circumstances is unique. The nature of the story, the complexity of the problem, the seriousness of making an ethical mistake—all these factors, and many others, will enter into each decision.

The ethical aspects of these judgments can be hard to separate from other journalistic concerns: from news judgment to questions of style and emphasis. So what is the ethical reporter to do? What guide can she or he use to make these judgments?

A STATEMENT OF PRINCIPLES

The many differences in standards don't mean that there is no common ground when it comes to journalistic ethics. In fact, most journalists would agree on certain broad ethical principles. The most widely accepted of these principles were set out in the American Society of Newspaper Editors' (A.S.N.E.) Statement of Principles in 1975.[2] They are responsibility, freedom of the press, independence, truth and accuracy, fair play, and impartiality.

Journalism changes over time, and there have been many changes since the editors proclaimed these principles. Scores of major newspapers have closed down or merged since then. Television has, in many ways, taken over from the printed press as the predominant news medium.

As a result of these and other changes, the ethical standards of journalism have frequently had to be reinterpreted. Practices that most responsible news organizations would have shunned twenty years ago (revealing the details of politicians' sex lives, for example) have become commonplace today. Nonetheless, the basic principles of journalistic ethics remain the same. They are still your best guide to making the ethical judgments a journalist needs to make.

RESPONSIBILITY

In the words of the A.S.N.E. statement, the press has "a particular responsibility" in U.S. society. "[J]ournalism demands of its practitioners not only industry and knowledge but also the pursuit of a standard of integrity proportionate to the journalist's singular obligation."

KINDS OF RESPONSIBILITIES • The journalist's first responsibility is to his or her audience. But the press has broader responsibilities as well: responsibilities to the society as a whole, and to the democratic system itself. To function at all, a democratic system requires an informed public, and it is the job of the press to inform that public. According to the A.S.N.E., in fact, "The primary purpose of gathering and distributing news and opinion is to serve the general welfare by informing people and enabling them to make judgments on the issues of the time." This purpose should govern the news judgment of reporters and editors alike.

PRIORITIES • Journalists need to maintain a sense of proportion in what they report, and how they report it. If the news media as a whole focus their attention and coverage on a particular event or issue, the public will focus on it too. It will gain a greater importance just from the fact that it's being covered so heavily. By the same token, if the news media ignore or downplay an issue, the public is likely to ignore it as well. Journalists need to fight the temptation to sensationalize the news, and to seek out and emphasize dramatic or lurid stories at the expense of more significant, but also more complex and less journalistically "sexy," events and issues.

Some critics point to recent coverage of crime as an example of what can happen when the press fails to keep a sense of proportion. Crime is a very alluring journalistic subject. It gets the public's juices flowing, provides plenty of human interest, and lots of dramatic pictures. Crime stories have always been a staple of local news, but in 1993 and 1994 it was frequently treated as a major national story as well.

For many years, violent crime had been only one of many issues ranked somewhere on the lists of concerns troubling the American people, as demonstrated by public-opinion polls. In the spring and summer of 1994, however, it leaped to the top. Suddenly, crime had become the single most important worry on people's minds. This was true despite the fact that the amount of violent crime had actually decreased significantly the year before, and was apparently continuing to drop.

Why should public concern about crime go up, even when the danger of crime was going down? The most convincing explanation for this oddity was the fact that the media had been increasing its emphasis on violent crime, even while the numbers of those crimes had been dropping.

Steven Roberts of *U.S. News & World Report* suggested that much of the fault for this obsession rested with local television news, which regularly led off its coverage with "flashing red lights and yellow tape."[3] What's more, both the print and electronic media had recently been showering enormous attention on a series of particularly gruesome crimes, including the bloody knifing deaths for which the football star O. J. Simpson had been charged. And more than one new "reality-based" series, such as *Cops*, appeared on television, documenting the activities of police, whether investigating major crimes or responding to routine calls. Actual crime—as opposed to the fictional cops-and-robbers variety that has always been a staple of the movies and TV—seemed to be everywhere in the media. It is not surprising that, for many people, crime seemed to be everywhere in real life as well.

Press critics charged that the media were focusing attention on crime at the expense of more important issues, such as AIDS, the decline in the standard of living of middle-class Americans, a wasteful and ineffective welfare system, racial discrimination, poverty in the United States, starvation in Africa, and the war in Bosnia. As a result, the public was deprived of discussion of these issues.

Whatever you think the public's priorities should be, it is clear that the press plays a big role in establishing them. This is a responsibility that journalists must keep in mind. It is important that they keep a sense of proportion in what they cover, and exercise good judgment on how much attention they give to different issues. They must beware of concentrating on sensational stories at the expense of more pressing public concerns. If the press is to inform people and enable them "to make judgements on the issues of the time," it must first make some judgments of its own.

FREEDOM OF THE PRESS

Freedom of the press is a fundamental freedom guaranteed by the U.S. Constitution. Ultimately, the A.S.N.E. Statement of Principles declares, that freedom belongs not only to journalists, but to all the people. It exists because the nation's founders recognized that it was only through a free press that the people could be fully informed of what the government was doing. What's more, it was only through a free press that the public debate necessary for an effective democracy could be carried out.

RESISTING CENSORSHIP • Although press freedom is a right that belongs to the people, it is up to journalists to uphold that right, and to defend it. Journalists have an ethical duty to resist government censorship in any form. What's more, they should refuse to allow themselves to be threatened or bullied into serving as a kind of propaganda arm of the government at any level, whether national, state, or

Many feel that the press gives too much coverage to crime stories and other journalistically "sexy" events. Reports on the 1994–95 murder trial of O. J. Simpson dominated the news, often at the expense of other more pressing stories.

local. The press must beware of misleading the public in order to promote some "greater" patriotic or governmental goal. The press's first duty is to inform its audience, not to serve the purposes of government. If anything, it should be skeptical of those purposes, and suspicious of that government.

In the words of the A.S.N.E. statement, "The American press was made free not just to inform or just to serve as a forum for debate but also to bring an independent scrutiny to bear on the forces of power in society, including the conduct of official power at all levels of government."

BEING WORTHY OF PRESS FREEDOM • The special protections the press enjoys impose another duty as well—the need to be worthy of that freedom. Some people would even argue that when the press fails to live up to the obligations imposed by its privileges, it should be censored or restricted as a punishment. Military officials, for example, accused the press of being irresponsibly critical, and even unpatriotic, when it covered the war in Vietnam in the 1960s and 1970s. In response, the Pentagon drastically limited the freedom of the press to cover military actions in Grenada and Panama in the 1980s.

The media had to struggle against Pentagon policies in covering the Persian Gulf War as well. The military tried to limit journalists' access to the battlefields by insisting on a pool arrangement. Only a small number of newspeople were permitted in, and then only under the supervision of public affairs officers, who reviewed their copy before allowing it to be sent out. Most journalists covering the war took part in the pool, in the belief that even government-supervised access to the war zones was better than no access at all. A daring few set out on their own, in defiance of the official arrangement.

Media representatives continue to negotiate with

military authorities over guidelines for covering future conflicts. But journalists should never accept the idea that a loss of freedom is a suitable punishment for press abuses. Even an irresponsible press needs to be free from government interference.

Freedom of the press is indivisible. The experience of the press in other countries makes clear that once any news medium is censored, all are in danger. Journalists should always fight for the press's right to cover—and criticize—every aspect of the government.

INDEPENDENCE

Freedom from government interference is vital, but it is not enough. The press needs to protect its independence from other outside forces as well. The press cannot "bring an independent scrutiny to bear on the forces of power in the society" if it allows itself to be controlled or dominated by those forces.

PRESSURES ON THE PRESS • The news media is under constant pressure from all sorts of social and economic forces. From principals who seek to censor every word that appears in the school newspaper to big businesses that spend millions of dollars advertising on network television and seek to control any damaging information the press might tell the public.

Interest groups of all kinds, from doctors' organizations to professional sports teams, seek to assure favorable press coverage of their activities and to head off criticism. Such organizations undermine press independence in a variety of ways. They call up editors and publishers to complain about coverage they find objectionable. They threaten boycotts. They withdraw advertising dollars. On the other hand, advertisers sometimes hold out the promise of more business, if coverage is favorable. It is the obligation of journalists—reporters, editors, and publishers alike—to resist such efforts in every way they can.

This is not to say that no complaints made about the news media are justified. Many are. Press coverage is too often mistaken or unfair. Journalists should always listen to criticism, and be willing to correct abuses when they occur. But they must try to respond to the substance of outside criticism, and not to the pressure or blandishments of the powerful forces that make them.

PERSONAL RELATIONSHIPS • Not all the dangers to press independence are as direct as those posed by school principals, big advertisers, and noisy pressure groups. Some of the greatest threats come from personal relationships. Journalists get to know people they cover. Reporters who cover military affairs find themselves spending a lot of time with military officers. Those whose beat is the government spend most of their time with politicians. Those whose beat is crime become friendly with the police. Almost inevitably, they start seeing their beat largely through their sources' point of view. They come to sympathize with their sources' problems and to appreciate their accomplishments.

Sometimes, they even become friends with individual sources they are writing about. The well-known political writer Bob Will, for example, was a good friend of Nancy Reagan, even while writing many pieces praising her husband Ronald's policies and achievements. Will is a columnist who writes opinion, and can perhaps be excused on that ground, but such personal relationships jeopardize journalists' ability to view their sources critically and to report on them objectively. It is hard to criticize your friends in print. On a purely human level, you're afraid that you will damage your relationship.

Because of these dangers, you should do your best to remain aloof from the people you cover. At the very least, it's a good idea to inform your editor of any personal relationship that might interfere with your coverage of a story. Ask her or him to help decide whether you should continue on the story or not. Many editors believe that reporters should never cover a single beat too long, because of this very danger.

SEEKING THE PUBLIC'S TRUST • Press independence is important in and of itself. To the extent that journalists are influenced by outside forces, they are hampered from telling the whole truth to their readers. But simply being independent is not always enough. Journalists need to be seen to be independent as well.

Effective journalism depends on the trust of the public. What's the use of telling the truth if nobody believes you? If the public believes you are unduly influenced by personal relationships or powerful outside forces, they will not trust what you have to say.

TRUTH AND ACCURACY

The main ethical duty of the journalist can be stated very simply: It is to tell the truth. But the truth can be hard to find and difficult to recognize. At best, journalists find only bits and pieces of it—and much of that turns out to be wrong or misleading.

A realistic ethical standard cannot require that the journalist "tell the truth" in an absolute sense. It cannot demand that the journalist always be right, that every story be accurate and complete. But it can, and does, demand that the journalist strive to tell the truth as she or he believes it to be. Even belief is not enough. The journalist must have *reasonable cause* to believe what he or she reports. You may think something is true. You may even be convinced of it. But if you don't have sufficient evidence to back up your belief, you cannot ethically report it as a fact.

THE DIFFERENCE BETWEEN ACCURACY AND TRUTH • It might seem odd that the A.S.N.E. statement speaks of both accuracy and truth. Many people would assume that they are the same thing. But they are not. A story can be accurate, in the sense of containing only facts, and still be untrue, in the sense of misleading the reader.

Take, for example, the early news reports of a deadly incident that occurred in the troubled African nation of Rwanda in the late summer of 1994. The first brief stories that came out of Rwanda and were broadcast on U.S. radio and television reported that Rwandan government forces had shot to death two exiles who were being escorted back into the country by representatives of the U.N. Only later, in longer versions of the story in both the electronic and print media, were the reports fleshed out to include certain all-important details. Among them was the information that the two dead exiles were suspected by the Rwandan authorities of being war criminals, and they had been killed only when fleeing from border guards who had attempted to question them.

By omitting the latter facts, the first reports gave the impression that two innocent men had been shot in cold blood by murderous government troops. The more detailed stories that came later made the soldiers' actions seem somewhat more reasonable.

The first story was accurate, so far as it went. The two men were refugees, they were being escorted back into Rwanda by U.N. representatives, and they were killed by Rwandan soldiers. But the story was also untrue. It gave a false impression about the killings, and what they indicated about the nature of the Rwandan authorities.

OTHER PEOPLE'S LIES • A story that quotes a lie without calling it a lie, is lying in itself. Consider the following item that might appear in a local newspaper:

Governor Largemouth T. Basse kicked off his campaign for reelection today with a speech on the steps of the State Capitol Building. "I'm proud of my record as your governor," he declared to an estimated crowd of two hundred supporters. "Under my leadership, our state has enjoyed unprecedented growth and prosperity. New business investment has soared and two million new jobs have been created. Best of all, state income taxes and property taxes have been reduced across the board!"

If the reporter has quoted the governor correctly, the story is perfectly accurate. But is it true? A careless reader might believe that this story reported the "growth and prosperity" of the state's economy under Governor Basse's administration. He or she would be wrong. All the story actually reports, of course, is what the governor said. It is the governor who claims that the economy improved, not the news story.

Because of this possible confusion in the reader's mind, the journalist should do more than simply report the governor's claims. He or she should put them in some kind of context to avoid leaving a false impression. How much more depends on whether the governor was telling the truth.

VERIFICATION • If possible, the reporter should verify the governor's assertions and tell the reader whether they are true or false. This could be done in several ways. The reporter could call state economists. If the governor's figures are true, nothing else has to be done. If they are false, the true figures can be printed in the story, following the governor's claims. At the very least, the governor or his staff can be asked to provide figures to prove his claims. If they do not, this fact can be mentioned in the story.

Verification may not always be possible, however. The real figures may be unavailable, or there might not be time. Such stories usually have to be done on a tight deadline. The speech takes place at noon, and the paper goes to bed at three, at which time it will be too late to turn in fresh copy. There will obviously not be time to verify any facts or figures the governor may use in his speech, but there are other ways to handle the problem.

The reporter can offer Governor Basse's opponent a chance to give his version of the state's progress under the governor, to use as a balance. Or a disclaimer can be added to the story, making clear that there had been no chance to verify the governor's claims.

Like many other ethical standards, the need of the press to seek out the truth of claims they publish is a question of some debate. Some mainstream journalists would argue that the reporter's duty was only to report what the governor said, and to let the reader decide about the truth or falsehood of those comments. To do more, these journalists would argue, would be editorializing. Others, however, including James Hoyt of the University of Wisconsin School of Journalism and Mass Communications, believe that journalists should never knowingly repeat lies without challenging them.[4] The press's responsibility is to expose lies, not to participate in them.

The duty to expose lies is strongest when the lies are made by politicians attempting to fool the public. To pass on such lies without correcting them makes the press an accomplice in the deception of the public.

FAIR PLAY

As a journalist, you should play fair with everyone.

LISTENING TO THE PUBLIC • Your obligation starts with the public, to whom you owe an honest and fair presentation of the news. You also need to listen to the public: to hear their complaints and to consider what they say seriously. Read the "Letters to the Editor" in your own publication, take calls from readers who want to complain about something that you wrote. And take them seriously. They are after all, the people you're attempting to inform.

Your first response to criticism from the public may be to become defensive, and to dismiss the complaint out of hand. After all, you know how accurate and fair you are, don't you? What does the reader know? Well, the reality is that you don't know you are not always fair. No human being is. And you are not always the best judge of your own objectivity, either. Sometimes, the complaining reader can tell you something you didn't know about your work.

Even when you feel the reader is completely off base, it's good to listen. After all, journalism is a form of communication, and communication is a two-way street. The readers (or listeners, or viewers) of news are vital elements of your business as a journalist. Without them, there would be no need for you.

AVOIDING DECEPTION • Journalists should not deceive their sources about who they are and what they are doing. A reporter should not pretend to be something else in order to collect information. It

It is important for journalists to listen to their public.
The New York-based columnist Jimmy Breslin is said
to visit several bars, where many of his readers
express their opinions to him.

would be wrong, for example, for a reporter to claim to be a policeman in order to wheedle information out of witnesses to a crime. Or to pretend to be a fellow mourner in order to convince relatives at the funeral of some prominent figure to surrender personal information about the deceased.

Some journalists insist that reporters should always identify themselves to potential sources. Others argue that this is unnecessary. If a source mistakenly *assumes* that a reporter is someone else, and begins to talk for that reason, there is no positive obligation for the reporter to stop the flow of information. But even most journalists who see nothing wrong in letting potential sources deceive themselves would agree that reporters should not actually *lie* to them about who they are.

Playing fair with sources doesn't mean that you have to use information only in the way your source would want you to use it, however. The mother of a criminal suspect might tell a reporter how her son once beat up a robber in the hope that it will make the reporter (and ultimately the public) feel more sympathetic to the young man. But the reporter is free to use the incident in any way she or he chooses: in order to illustrate the suspect's history of violent behavior, for instance.

CONFIDENTIALITY • In general, the confidentiality of sources should be respected. If a source will only give you information on certain conditions—and you agree to those conditions—then you should keep your word. This includes the (hopefully) unusual case in which you agree to keep your source anonymous. As we discuss in another chapter, deals with sources are tricky, and they should be avoided when possible. But, when made, they should be kept.

Ethically, the trust between a reporter and source

is as vital as the trust between a reporter and the public. And, as a practical matter, journalists who violate the deals they make with sources soon find those sources drying up.

FAIRNESS TO SUBJECTS • You owe a different kind of fair play to those you write about. In the words of the A.S.N.E. statement, you need to "respect the rights of those involved in the news."

PRIVACY • Reporters sometimes need to poke and pry into the private lives and personal activities of people. But, in doing so, they should always remain aware of the humanity of those people and respect their rights and feelings.

BALANCE • A news writer is not omniscient. That is, he or she does not know everything. Within limits, news writers should try to assure that controversial negative information about a person or thing is balanced by positive information. When writing about a piece of proposed legislation, for example, try to include quotes or arguments from legislators on both sides of the issue. When reporting ethical or other accusations against anyone who claims to be innocent, try to include a response from the person, his lawyer, or a family member willing to come to his or her defense.

    Opinion writers, of course, don't need to be as concerned about balance as other journalists. Unlike straight news writers, they are free to "stack" their arguments. They can present whatever facts they choose, and leave it up to opposing opinion writers to present the facts that might damage their position.

LIBEL • The most basic element of fairness to the people you write about is accuracy. Even the most negative story, about the most despised subject, must not libel them. That is, it must not make false accusations against them. The U.S. Supreme Court defines libel as writing that "tends to expose" someone "to public hatred, shame, obloquy, contumely, odium, contempt, ridicule, aversion, ostracism, degradation, or disgrace, or to induce an evil opinion of one in the minds of right-thinking persons, and to deprive one of their confidence and friendly intercourse in society."[5]

Libel is a legal offense, and people who feel that they have been libeled can sue. In general, however, libel does not include statements of opinion, as opposed to claims of fact. You are free to say that you believe Senator Bigpockets to be an "unprincipled jerk," as well as an incompetent public servant, but you must not accuse him of taking bribes he did not take.

The law of libel is applied differently to different kinds of people. It is relatively easy to step over the legal bounds in making accusations against ordinary men and women, who may appear in the newspaper only because newsworthy events happen around them. Entertainers, sports stars, and other public figures who have deliberately sought public attention are harder to libel. They can usually win a libel suit only by proving that the attack was published with "actual malice." That means that the writer either knew that the claim was untrue or published it with "reckless disregard" of whether it was true or not.[6]

Politicians—public officials and those seeking public office—are the hardest of all to libel. In practice, you can publish almost anything, however reckless or outrageous, against a politician with very little risk of being sued successfully. This is because the First Amendment is very protective of political speech, in order to assure a vigorous and free debate over public issues. If it were easy for government officials to sue people who criticized them, it would be easy for the government to silence the press.

Journalists, however, should not beware of libel primarily because they are worried about being sued. Libel is ethically wrong, as well as legally wrong. Good journalists would never knowingly libel anyone, even if they thought they could get away with it.

THE RIGHT TO RESPOND • Journalists should never be reluctant to publish accurate and relevant damaging information against people who have done wrong. When accusing individuals of illegal or otherwise dishonorable acts, however, you should give them a chance to answer the accusation. Ideally, this should be before the accusation is published. You should attempt to speak to the subject, explain the accusation, and ask what he or she has to say about it. If this is impractical, a chance to respond should be offered at "the earliest opportunity."

CORRECTING MISTAKES • Finally, says the A.S.N.E., journalists must "stand accountable to the public for the fairness and accuracy of their news reports." Even when you're convinced that everything you've written is absolutely true and fair, not everyone will agree with you. What's more, they will sometimes be right. No matter how good a reporter you are, and how careful you try to be, you're going to make mistakes. Fair play requires that those mistakes get corrected, promptly and prominently.

Ideally, in fact, the correction should be displayed as prominently as the original error. Unfortunately, the decision about whether to make a correction, and where that correction will be displayed, is often out of the reporter's hands. It is up to the editor. But a reporter who realizes that she or he had made a mistake can, and should, make sure that the editor is informed. Reporters frequently neglect to do this. It can be embarrassing to admit a mistake, and some editors are not eager to hear about them, either. But correcting mistakes is a necessary part of ethical journalism.

IMPARTIALITY

To be impartial means not to take sides. As a standard of journalistic ethics, it applies primarily to the writing of straight news. When writing opinion you would not want to avoid taking sides, even if you could.

This is perhaps the most controversial principle of journalistic ethics, and the one that has changed the most since the newspaper editors published their statement in 1975. Some people still believe that news reporters should strive to be completely objective in their work. Charges that they are not—that the press is politically and culturally biased—are leveled against journalists from every direction. Because of the special role this issue plays in the way people view the press, we will deal with it in more detail in the chapter titled "Dealing with Bias."

HOW ETHICAL IS AMERICAN JOURNALISM TODAY?

This is not the place for a long examination of the state of journalistic ethics today. It should be noted, however, that American journalism often falls sadly short of the goals set forth in the A.S.N.E. Statement of Principles.

Much of what appears in even the most responsible press is inaccurate to some degree, and a lot of what is accurate is misleading. Errors are sometimes not corrected at all, and when they are, the correction is seldom displayed as prominently as the original error. Most media routinely repeat the claims of business leaders, government authorities, and other politicians, without regard to whether they are true.

Many of the failures of the modern press do not result from incompetence or corruption, however. They result from the fact that journalists are human beings. They are not infallible, nor are they supermen and superwomen with X-ray vision for the truth. They are just ordinary people trying to understand and report incredibly complex events. Much of the information they receive comes from unreliable or even deliberately deceptive sources. What's more, they are almost always working on unrealistically short deadlines. A certain amount of carelessness and a certain number of mistakes are inevitable.

It is the duty of every journalist, however, to be aware of the ethics of his or her profession; to take them seriously; and to attempt to live up to them, to the best of his or her ability.

SIX

DEALING WITH BIAS

Mainstream American journalism attempts to be as objective and impartial as possible in reporting the news. In recent years, however, it has come under increasingly intense fire for being just the opposite.

The public complains that the press is biased. They are convinced that journalists slant the news, and fill their reports with propaganda instead of facts. The loudest and most frequent complaints come from conservatives who complain that the press is too politically liberal, but liberals protest that the press is far too conservative.

Journalists like to respond that, since they're being attacked from both sides, they must be doing a fair job. If readers think the press is biased, it's not because the press publishes propaganda. It's because they refuse to publish propaganda. Many readers, the journalists say, actually want propaganda—propaganda that supports the readers' side of every issue. When they get objective reporting instead, the readers see it as biased against them.

This is a comfortable belief for journalists, but it's

not entirely convincing. After all, the fact that almost everybody thinks journalists slant the news is hardly proof that they don't do it.

More and more journalists are beginning to recognize that they probably do slant the news to some extent, however unintentionally. And they're beginning to wonder what they can—or should—do about it.

HOW BIAS SHOWS ITSELF

It goes without saying that a journalist should never falsify a story, or deliberately misstate facts in order to fool the reader. No honorable journalist would ever do such a thing. But, even when the facts are presented with scrupulous accuracy, stories are still sometimes slanted to present a subject more favorably or unfavorably.

This is sometimes done deliberately in order to influence the readers' opinions, but it can also happen unintentionally. And, for honest journalists, that's where the real danger lies. News writers often let bias slip into their stories through carelessness, sometimes because they don't recognize their own opinions and prejudices.

This happens in two different ways. The first is through the choices the writer makes about which facts or details to use in the story. The second is through an often unconscious choice of verbs and adjectives.

Take three versions of the same news story about a fictitious Republican budget proposal in an imaginary American state. All three stories present the same basic facts and figures, but in ways that give a very different impression of the proposal being discussed.

REPUBLICANS PROPOSE
BUDGET

Republican leaders from both houses of the New Heartland state legislature today announced an alternative to the budget put forward last week by Democratic governor Robert Crandall. The Republican proposal would provide less state money for welfare, education, and social programs, but more for programs aimed at controlling crime, and for promoting state businesses and tourism.

The Republicans propose spending $50 million less on the state university system, and $25 million less on assistance to local school boards. AFDC and other welfare expenditures would be held to some $100 million less than proposed by the Democrats by tightening eligibility requirements for several programs.

Under the Republican alternative, state salary expenditures would actually be reduced by $10 million from the current year's expenses, a reduction they say could be accomplished by allowing attrition to eliminate roughly 200 state jobs.

The Republicans would spend $50 million more on the State Police agency, and increase state aids to local law-enforcement agencies by a similar amount. In addition, the Republicans want to spend $15 million to establish a state government agency to promote international sales of goods produced here. They would also spend $8 million more than the Democrats on encouraging tourism, including a new $5 million campaign promot-

ing state attractions on television in neighboring states.

Overall, the Republican proposal would mean an increase of $750 million over the current year's budget, which would be $150 million less than the increase proposed by the Democrats. Both budgets, however, would mean an increase in state income taxes for the typical taxpayer.

The second version of the story presents the same facts in a generally positive way:

REPUBLICANS PROPOSE SAVINGS

Republican leaders from both houses of the New Heartland state legislature announced a new budget proposal today, designed to hold down state spending in the coming year. The Republican proposal is a less expensive alternative to the massive budget put forward last week by the Democratic governor, Robert Crandall.

The Republicans would reduce spending on some big welfare and social programs, while holding down education costs. At the same time, they would beef up spending to fight crime, and provide funds to boost business and tourism in the state. One hundred million dollars would be chopped from the Democrats' proposed welfare budget by toughening up eligibility requirements for many state programs. In addition, the Republicans would chop $50 million from the huge boost the Democrats propose giving to the state university system, while snipping $25 million from gifts to local school boards.

The Republican proposal would actually slice $10 million from the state's salary expenditures by eliminating the jobs of roughly 200 bureaucrats.

On the other hand, the Republicans plan to step up the state's war on crime by providing $100 million more to state and local law-enforcement agencies. They would also budget $15 million to establish a new agency to promote the international sales of goods produced in the state, at a cost of only $15 million, including start-up costs and first-year expenses. They would also spend $8 million more than the Democrats to encourage the state's tourism, including a sum that would provide for a brand-new $5 million campaign to promote state attractions on television in neighboring states.

Overall, the Republican proposal would mean an increase of only $750 million over the current year's budget, a full $150 million less than the increase proposed by the Democrats. It would also mean a significantly lower increase in state income taxes for the typical taxpayer.

A third version presents the imaginary Republican proposal in a much different light:

REPUBLICANS SEEK TO CUT PROGRAMS

Republican leaders from both houses of the New Heartland state legislature announced their own budget proposal today, an alternative to the one put forward last week by the Democratic governor, Robert Crandall. The Republican proposal cuts state

87

education, welfare, and social services, while providing substantially more state money for police and new subsidies to private business.

The Republicans would deprive an undisclosed number of families of $100 million in welfare benefits, by eliminating them from programs for which they are now eligible. They would also eliminate some 200 state jobs, mostly by attrition, in an effort to save some $10 million in salary expenses.

Among the biggest and most important programs to suffer under the Republican proposal would be education. The Republican budget proposes to deny the state university system some $50 million in planned assistance, and to strip away some $25 million in aid to the state's troubled local school boards.

Some $100 million of the money these cuts might save would be used up in grants to the state and local police agencies. Another $15 million would be spent to establish an entirely new state government agency to promote foreign sales of goods produced in the state. The Republicans also propose spending $8 million more than the Democrats on tourism promotion, $5 million of which would be spent on out-of-state television ads.

Despite the many cuts in major programs, the Republican proposal would mean an increase of $750 million over the current year's budget, a mere $150 million less than the increase in the Democrats' budget, which expands, rather than cuts, many state programs. Both budgets call for tax increases.

None of the three stories expresses a direct opinion for or against the Republican proposal. The writers of each could defend the accuracy of every line in their story. And they might all, in fact, have intended to be scrupulously accurate and fair in their reporting. And yet, while the first version is relatively neutral, the other two are not. The second version of the story is essentially positive, if not actually supportive of the Republican proposal. The third is clearly negative.

How can this be? How can the same facts be slanted in different directions by writers trying to be accurate and objective? The answer lies mostly in the choice of the words the writers use to describe the budget proposal and its effects. Consider a few examples:

In the positive version of the story, the Republican proposal "is designed to hold down state spending." In the negative version, it is described as cutting "state education, welfare, and social services." Both statements are, presumably, true. Yet "hold[ing] down state spending" is a goal that readers are likely to sympathize with—particularly readers who pay taxes in that state. Cutting education and other state "services," however, is a much more controversial effort.

In the positive story, the Republican proposal includes money to "beef up spending to fight crime," while in the negative version the money "would be used up in grants to the state and local police agencies." "Beef[ing] up spending" sounds like a strong, constructive thing to do, and "fight[ing] crime" is a goal every honest citizen can applaud. "Us[ing] up" money in grants to police "agencies" sounds much weaker, if not actually wasteful.

In the positive story, the Republicans "chop" $100 million "from the Democrats' proposed welfare budget by toughening up eligibility requirements for many state programs." In the negative version, they "deprive an undisclosed number of families of $100 million in welfare benefits by eliminating them from programs." Here, more than just a choice of words is involved. In the positive story, the Republicans are described as taking an ax to an inanimate and unfeeling object—the Democratic "welfare budget." In the negative story, they are taking an action that will hurt living, breathing, and possibly already suffering, human beings.

The stories also end on very different notes. The positive version points to the "significantly lower tax increase[s]" proposed in the Republican plan, while the negative version emphasizes that "both plans" would mean higher taxes.

There is no way for a writer to avoid making choices like those made differently in each of the three stories. And each choice made, in each story, could be fairly defended as journalistically sound. And yet, noting the differences, it may be easier to understand why so many readers assume that the press is biased.

THE IDEAL OF IMPARTIALITY

Historically, the idea of an impartial press is relatively new. During the first hundred years of American journalism and even after, news writers made no effort to keep their opinions out of their reporting. Most nineteenth-century newspapers, in fact, were founded explicitly to promote the opinions of a political party, or even of a particular owner and publisher.

There were Democratic papers, and Republican papers. Papers that supported slavery, and papers that supported abolition, prohibition, the free coinage of silver, or any other cause imaginable. They had names like the *Torch of Liberty*, the *Cleveland Democrat*, and the *Richland Center Republican and Observer*. Such papers openly—and proudly—trumpeted the causes they championed. Editorial and news columns alike were filled with the most blatant propaganda.

The famous debates between Abraham Lincoln and Stephen Douglas, for instance, were reported very differently by the Republican and Democratic press. When Lincoln's supporters hoisted Lincoln up on their shoulders after one debate, the Republican papers reported that Honest Abe had scored such a glorious victory that the ecstatic crowd had borne him off in triumph. Democratic papers, on the other hand, reported that Lincoln had been so overcome by the verbal beating Douglas had administered that he was too weak to walk and had to be carried from the scene.

The best of the nineteenth- and early twentieth-century reporters believed in facts, but they also believed using those facts to make a point. They made no effort to hide their biases, they prided themselves on them. "I am not a scientist, " declared the great muckraker Lincoln Steffens. "I am a journalist . . . I wanted to move and convince."[1]

By the mid-twentieth century, however, a very different standard had been established. News writers were not supposed to take sides. They were not supposed to "move and convince." Instead, they were expected to keep their personal views and feelings out of their work. Like doctors and lawyers, they were supposed to remain cool and dispassionate, objective.

Why the change? In the old days, it didn't cost much to run a newspaper. Every city of any size had several newspapers, each with its own point of view. A big city might have ten or more major papers. Even

During the nineteenth century, news writers did little to hide their biases. Lincoln Steffens, known as a "muckraker," wrote very moving pieces aimed at fighting social injustice.

many small towns had two or three. Readers could pick the one that they agreed with. By the 1960s and 1970s, that had changed. Newspapers were going under at a terrific rate, or being swallowed up by other papers. Even the biggest cities had only a handful of major papers, and most small cities had only one.

Newspapers could no longer afford to appeal to a small audience of like-minded readers. In order to appeal to everybody, not just those readers who agreed with them, they had to convince readers to trust what they told them. And that meant they had to convince them that they were no longer publishing propaganda, but the objective truth.

Papers tried to do this by building a wall between their editorial columns and their news pages. They would still publish editorials and opinion pieces, but only when they were clearly labeled as such. Opinion would be banned from their news reporting altogether. So it was that objectivity became the goal and promise of the serious journalist.

CHANGING STANDARDS

But today, journalistic standards are beginning to change again. News reporters are still expected to be accurate, and not to let their opinions get in the way of a fair and balanced presentation of the facts. But editors are no longer fighting as hard as they once did to keep all opinion out of the news columns. "The newspaper . . . where reporters bend over backwards to be objective is becoming a thing of the past," a reporter recently explained to a television interviewer. "Fair? We'll always try to be fair and accurate. But objective? Not so much anymore."[2]

One reason for the retreat from objectivity is the recognition that total objectivity may be impossible to maintain. Can a reporter witness starving children wracked with cholera in Somalia or Rwanda and remain unmoved? Should he or she really write about such things coldly, letting no sense of pain or outrage come through? "The business is a subjective business," says investigative reporter Paul Rodriguez of the *Washington Times.* "Your ultimate hope is to be accurate. In that accuracy comes a fairness."[3]

Another reason for the changing standard is the

fact that many readers have never believed journalists' claims of objectivity anyway. No matter how hard journalists strove to be objective, many readers remained convinced that they were hopelessly biased.[4]

Some journalists believe that, as long as they're going to be damned for bias anyway, they might as well let their real biases show. And editors are more willing than they used to be to let the reporters' personal responses to events slip into their stories. What's more, analysis is becoming a regular feature in more and more news articles.

TO BE OR NOT TO BE—OBJECTIVE?

So, what are you, as a news writer, supposed to do? The rules are in the process of changing, and what the standards of the future will be is still unclear. In the meantime, you should probably approach straight news stories as impartially as you can. Most important, you must not let your personal feelings and opinions dictate the choices you make in deciding what facts to report and how you report them.

The key word in the last sentence is dictate. The reality is that your personal feelings and opinions will always influence the way you approach a story, and the choices you make in writing it. You bring your whole background, knowledge, and personality to your job as a reporter, and to every story you write. The way you see the world is bound to affect the way you see a story.

This is not entirely a bad thing. After all, it is your knowledge and experience that make you a reporter. Good reporters have to sift through the information they receive, and make many kinds of judgments about it. It is up to them to separate, as best they

In the middle

ROTHCO

can, the important from the trivial and the true from the false. A reporter who simply recorded whatever was put in front of him or her would be far too naive and gullible to be a reliable judge of these things.

When writing news analysis, opinion can play a more direct part in your story. In fact, interpretation relies very heavily on the personal opinions of the reporter, and interpretation is what news analysis is all about.

Ultimately, it is up to the editor to make sure that the public knows the difference between the various kinds of newswriting. "Sound practice," declares the A.S.N.E., "demands a clear distinction for the reader between news reports and opinion." Stories that contain the latter "should be clearly identified."

You don't need to keep your personal opinions from influencing what you write, even when you're writing straight news. You couldn't do that, anyway. But what you must do is to recognize that influence, and make sure that it assists your journalistic judgment instead of distorting it.

PART
FOUR

PUTTING IT ALL
TOGETHER

SEVEN

WRITING LEADS

In the course of collecting information, conducting interviews, and going about the other chores of a journalist, it's easy to forget that the most important part of our job is to communicate what we find to our readers.

To write the story.

We must never forget that newswriting is just that: writing. Many news writers are a little apologetic about this part of their craft. When asked what they do for a living, they identify themselves as reporters, columnists, reviewers, or whatever—never as writers. But in fact there is no fundamental distinction between what news writers do and what is done by their more literary brothers and sisters who write fiction and essays. There are, in fact, only two significant differences. News writers are more limited in what they write about, and usually have less time to do it. But good writing is good writing, whether it appears in a book or a newspaper.

Inevitably, the moment comes when it's time to sit down and begin to write the story. In daily reporting, that moment comes sooner. In investigative reporting, where a story might be researched for days, weeks, or even months, it comes later. But it always comes.

HOOKING THE READER

The beginning of a news story is called the lead. This is the reader's introduction to the story. Some leads are simple statements of fact. Others are more elaborate and imaginative.

A lead can be as short as one sentence, or as long as several paragraphs. The right length depends on what kind of lead it is, and the length of the story itself. Obviously, a four-paragraph story can't afford a two-paragraph introduction. On the other hand, a major feature, running to a thousand words or more, might devote more than a hundred of them to a good lead.

The lead is important to any news story, but it is especially crucial to human interest features, columns, and other pieces that are not primarily straight news. Readers come to a newspaper or other news source for a simple and obvious reason— they want to find out what's happened. A straight news story attracts readers because of the news itself. Because of the event being reported, they are either interested or they are not. If they want to know what happened, they need to read the story.

For features or opinion pieces there's no such built-in need. People have to be persuaded to read them. A good lead can do that—attracted by the headline, or just out of curiosity, potential readers may glance at your story. If the lead excites them, they will continue to read. But if the lead is boring or clumsily written, they will skip over it and go on to something else. They never get the benefit of the exhaustive research you have done. They will never find out how important your story really is, or how well you have written it.

But a good lead catches the readers' attention, and makes them want to read on. For that reason, a lead is sometimes referred to as the "hook." It catches the reader the way a hook catches a fish. It is up to the body of the piece to reel the reader in.

The requirements for a good lead are much the same as the requirements for good newswriting in general. Much of the following advice about writing leads should apply equally well to the body of your story. As we've said, good writing is good writing is good writing.

RELEVANCE

A good lead needs to be more than catchy. It needs to be relevant. It does no good to attract a reader to a feature under false pretenses. There's no point in writing an entertaining lead about baseball if your piece is going to be about economics, or a grim description of a forest fire to introduce an upbeat story about the Special Olympics.

Some leads, as we will see, tease the reader. They are deliberately misleading about what the subject is going to be. But before the lead is over, the reader should have a good sense of what the story is going to be about, and whether or not he or she is likely to be interested in it.

TONE

The best leads introduce the tone and style of the piece, as well as the subject. They attract the readers who will be interested in what is to come and gently warn off those who will not. Fiction writers have known how to do this for a long time. Consider the following classic examples:

Call me Ishmael. Some years ago—never mind how long precisely—having little or no money in my purse, and nothing particular to interest me on shore, I thought I would sail about a little and see the watery part of the world. It is a way I have of driving off the spleen and regulating the circulation. Whenever I find myself growing grim about the mouth; whenever it is damp, drizzly November in my soul; whenever I find myself involuntarily pausing before coffin warehouses, and bringing up the rear of every funeral I meet; and especially whenever my hypos get such an upper hand of me, that it requires a strong moral principle to prevent me from deliberately stepping into the street, and methodically knocking people's hats off— then, I account it high time to get to sea as soon as I can.[1]

Could there be a more promising introduction to a sea adventure than that? And yet, this lead implies more than a simple yarn about the sea. It is brilliant because, besides getting the reader's attention, it gives intriguing clues to the kind of story the writer is about to tell. The long complex sentences, and the reference to the Biblical character Ishmael, make clear that this will be no simple-minded entertainment. It will demand thought from the reader. At the same time, the gloomy references to coffin warehouses and funerals suggest that something darker than a simple adventure story is in store. It is, in fact, the opening of one of the greatest American novels ever written: Herman Melville's *Moby Dick*.

Sometimes, everything you need to do in a lead can be done in a single sentence: "He was born with a gift of laughter and a sense that the world was mad."[2] This is the opening sentence of Rafael Sabatini's *Scaramouche*, one of the most popular of all adventure novels. Without knowing anything else about the book that follows, this sentence alone would tell you that the book's hero will be a dashing and colorful figure, the kind of man you would look forward to spending a few hundred pages with. What's more, it assures you that the author was born with a gift of language and a sense of how to entertain. It has a lilt to it that promises that what follows will be a lot of fun. In the case of *Scaramouche*, the promise is kept.

FINDING IDEAS FOR LEADS

The leads for some stories seem to come naturally. They are just *there*, in your mind, when you sit down to write your story. But at other times you have to look for them. Sometimes, you have to look very hard.

You may know what you want to say. What the facts are, and how they fit together to make up the story you want to tell. But you don't know how to introduce the information, how to grab the readers' interest and focus their attention on what you have to say. In such cases, you have to search for your lead. You have to rummage around in your story—and in your own imagination—to find just the right hook to catch the reader. And it really can be like a search. It is as though the lead is already there, somewhere, and you have to seek it out. When you do, you have a real feeling of discovery. Eureka! I have found it!

SUMMARIZE

U.S. forces enter Haiti today as a peaceful rather than hostile force after President Clinton's negotiators Sunday night barely averted a U.S. invasion.[3]

The Gramercy Ground Squirrels won the championship with a 3–2 victory over the Capital Comets in the final game of the Midwest Regional Soccer Tournament in Detroit yesterday.

These are examples of what is known as the hard lead. A simple summary of what your story is about, the hard lead is the traditional opening for a straight news story. When the event you are describing is really important, as in the first example above, this can be the most dramatic lead of all. Yet when the event is less compelling, as in the second example, it still remains the most useful possible lead from the readers' point of view. It gives them the information they need most right up front, and allows them to decide for themselves whether to read on for more detail.

GET RIGHT TO THE HEART OF YOUR STORY

To write a summary lead, you need to understand what your story is really about, and why readers might be interested in it.

"President Johnson announced tonight that he will not seek re-election for another term." This was the startling lead of the front-page article of the *Chicago Tribune*, on April 1, 1968.[4] In this case, the heart of the story was obvious. At other times, it's not so clear.

If you're having trouble finding your lead, it may be because you don't really understand your own story. What is the meat of that story? What is the central fact, or the most important element of it? Is it a breaking event? A fire? A visit by a foreign dignitary? The naming of the varsity football team? If so, the lead "writes itself."

Sometimes, however, you need to think harder to figure out what the real meat of your story really is. Why are people going to be interested in it? Why should they be?

If you're reporting a speech by the chairwoman of the local school board, what is the most important thing she said? That is your natural lead. If you're reporting the results of a poll, what is the most significant—or surprising—finding of the poll? That, too, is a natural lead.

PAINT A SCENE

Sometimes a description of a landscape can serve as a kind of visual introduction to your story.

> *Fresno, Calif.—From afar, the furrows of vineyards here are an endless mosaic of tan desert dust and the irregular black outlines of raisins.*
>
> *It is a dramatic but dismal sight. Weeks after the traditional end of the harvest, raisins still remain unharvested, growing moldy in the dry San Joaquin Valley breeze . . .*[5]

This was the brief, but evocatively bleak opening of a Karen Brandon piece about the shortage of vineyard harvesters in California, brought about by firm efforts to stop workers from illegally entering the state from Mexico.

BRING IT "UP CLOSE AND PERSONAL"

In the example below, Bill Keller carried scene painting one step further by adding a human being to the landscape, a human being deeply involved in the events his story would be about. Keller's subject was the bloody fighting between Armenians and Azerbaijanis in a distant corner of the former Soviet Union, known as Nagorno-Karabakh. Most of his readers would not know where Nagorno-Karabakh was, and wouldn't care. Keller needed a way to bring readers into his story. He needed a lead that would allow the reader to relate to this obscure conflict. He needed a way to personalize the struggle, and to show that his piece wasn't just a battle report, but a story about people.

He found his lead in a simple coincidence of architecture and geography:

> From the windows of her living room, Galya Israelyan can look down over the rooftops of this Armenian village, out to the green and gold mountains and the clearing where a few days ago her husband, Ruben, was shot dead.
>
> He was 32 years old and the father of five, including a newborn daughter, when he became a casualty in the Soviet Union's fiercest and most intractable nationalist feud in recent years.[6]

NARRATE

As we have already seen, fiction writers have long been masters of effective leads. Many techniques can be learned from them. Not the least is to open with a narration of an event that is central to the story to come. This was the case, for example, with a 1994 *Time* magazine piece about the effects of the assassination of Mexican presidential candidate Luis Donaldo Colosio. Written by Bruce W. Nelan, it opened with a graphic account of the assassination itself.

"The assassin stood unnoticed in the crowd," the article began. It went on to describe the setting, with Luis Donaldo Colosio speaking to 3,000 poor people in "a ramshackle neighborhood near Tijuana's airport." Finished with the speech, the candidate had "waded into the crush to shake hands," when "the assassin edged up behind him, thrust a .38 cal. pistol at his head and fired." After describing the effects of the first shot, the opening paragraph concluded, "the gunman leaned over and fired another bullet into the fallen man's stomach."[7]

In this example, the scene was probably a reconstruction, put together from TV film and witnesses' accounts of the event. There is no indication that the author himself was present. If the author had been present, the use of the first person could have added authority to the description of the scene.

Few subjects offer such sensational—and violent—opportunities for leads as this example does. But opening scenes do not have to be sensational. They can just as well describe quiet, unremarkable moments that simply illustrate some key aspect of the subject you are writing about.

GO FOR THE DRAMA

Leads need to be relevant, but they don't need to be dull. That's true even when you're afraid the subject of the piece might *seem* dull to most readers. Readers don't always know what's going to interest them. The best way to attract them may be to point out a fact that emphasizes the drama in what might ordinarily seem to be a dry and undramatic subject.

That drama can often be found in the emotions raised by the subject under discussion. Human emotion adds interest even to subjects most readers would ordinarily dismiss as obscure. The education policy known as outcome-based education (or OBE), for example, is a subject most readers would consider pretty dry and academic. Even most parents. Yet, faced with writing a story on it for the *Milwaukee Journal*, Jo Sandin found this dramatic lead:

> *The death threat came on a quiet Sunday afternoon while teacher Jeff Stern was playing a game with his children at their Sun Prairie home.*
> *"If you value your life, you'll stop teaching OBE," a man's voice said.*[8]

The fact that someone felt strongly enough about this seemingly obscure educational policy to threaten to kill a teacher probably came as a surprise to most readers. As a lead, the account of the death threat was designed to spark their interest, and make them want to read on to discover what made this esoteric academic fad so controversial.

SHOCK

A startling fact can sometimes be used to grab the reader's attention. Consider the following opening to a *Los Angeles Times* opinion piece by Paul Shrivastava:

> *Each year we generate more than 150 million tons of garbage, in the form of 250 million tires, 2 billion disposable batteries,*

*28 billion glass bottles and jars, 50 million
tons of paper and 18 billion disposable dia-
pers.*[9]

Shrivastava followed that opening with a plea for
renewable products and packaging. If that collection
of astonishing statistics didn't make readers pay
attention to what he had to say, probably nothing
would.

PUT YOUR STORY IN CONTEXT

The significance of some stories is obvious, but others take some explaining. In some stories, the event
being reported is only important because of a particular political or social context. The lead offers a
chance to put the news you are reporting in that context, to explain its importance to your readers.

Political polls are being taken all the time. They
keep track of public opinion on issues and political
figures. In and of themselves, most of these polls are
unimportant. But some carry special meaning, either
because their results are surprising, or because they
reflect a significant trend. Richard Benedetto introduced a report on the results of a poll of people's
attitude toward President Bill Clinton this way:

*Jobs are up, inflation's low. And, despite
foreign fumbles, the USA is at peace.*
*By every traditional measure, President
Clinton should be riding high in the polls, yet
recent surveys find growing disquiet with his
presidency.*[10]

The lead indicated that the story that followed
was more than a report of the poll itself. Polls are

snapshots of public opinion. Viewed by themselves, they say little more than what people are thinking at that particular moment. They can change overnight, and completely turn around in a matter of weeks. But Benedetto's lead made clear that the real story was not what people were thinking about the president at that moment, but why they were thinking it.

The lead kept readers from looking at the poll in isolation. It urged them to consider the results in a broader and more interesting context. Why should public opinion of the president be so low at a time when things were going pretty well in the country at large? What did this mean for Clinton's presidency? This made the poll more than a snapshot in time. It turned it into a question mark over the president's future.

GIVE IT A LOCAL HOOK

The following lead, which appeared in a local paper in Wausau, Wisconsin, introduced a story reporting a state supreme court decision on the cleanup of Superfund toxic waste sites.

Instead of going right to the subject of the story—the state supreme court decision—the lead began by putting what would follow in a local context. It gave the paper's hometown readers a local reason to care.

Whether Wausau, Schofield and other municipalities and businesses have any insurance coverage for their $7 million portion of the $11.5 million Holtz-Krause landfill cleanup is uncertain following a State Supreme Court decision Thursday.[11]

This is what is sometimes called a "local hook."

INVITE THE READER INTO YOUR STORY

Use of the second person can be an effective device for some kinds of leads. By addressing the reader directly, you invite the reader into your story and enlist his or her interest in what you are saying.

One way to do this is to provoke the reader's imagination:

> *Imagine it is midwinter, you are strolling through the local grocer's produce aisle and dreaming of summer—when tomatoes aren't green and oranges aren't yellow.*
> *This winter, part of your dream may come true.*[12]

The above was the lead to a newspaper piece on a bioengineered tomato, one that could be grown and delivered fresh all over the country throughout the year.

ASK A QUESTION

How do you get the reader to think about something?

Well, one way is to do what I just did. Ask a question. There is no more direct way to engage the reader than by asking a direct question.

Questions can be used effectively, in a variety of ways. One that personally involves the readers can relate your story to their lives. You might start a piece on pension plans or other retirement issues with a question like this: "How much money will you need to be secure and comfortable once your working life is over? And will you have it?"

Most people are concerned about their financial future. But many have never faced that question in such stark, and simple, terms. For a lot of people who are not already planning for their retirement, it will be a frightening thought. Seeing the question on the page will shake them up and make them wonder: Yes, how much money will I need? And where will I get it? With their minds stimulated to start wondering about their financial security—and maybe worry about it, too—they will be inclined to read on to see what you have to tell them.

But opening questions do not have to be so personal, nor do they have to relate the story to the readers' lives. They can be used simply to engage the reader's interest in a subject of more general concern. "Why do Mexican immigrants in Los Angeles tend to have more children than impoverished peasants living in Mexico City?" asked a *Time* magazine essay by Eugene Linden.[13]

The readers Linden was speaking to were neither Mexican peasants nor Mexican immigrants. They were ordinary Americans concerned about public issues like immigration and welfare costs. Having aroused the reader's curiosity with his question, Linden went on to discuss the relationship between population growth, poverty, and social benefits.

Gabriel Constans used a different sort of question to arouse his readers' interest in Aung San Suu Kyi, a person most of them had probably never heard of:

"Why," he asked, "would six Nobel Peace Prize winners and representatives of two Peace Prize–winning organizations travel to Thailand and Geneva to publicize the fate of a single woman in a country called Myanmar?"[14]

The reason, as Constans went on to explain, was that Suu Kyi was the imprisoned leader of a Burmese democracy movement that Constans believed might mark the beginning of the end for many tyrannical governments in Asia.

POSE A RIDDLE

A neat variation on the ask-a-question technique is to pose a riddle. Because of the humorous tone set by riddles, this technique is usually best suited for relatively insignificant, soft news stories. Here, for example, is how one reporter piqued readers' interest in a subject that, stated baldly, might have seemed both too dry and too inconsequential for most readers to bother reading about:

> *Senators steal them. Television cameras love them. News conferences feature them. They have proliferated around the Capitol like tourists in August.*
> *What are they?*[15]

The answer: charts, graphs, and other visual aids that Congresspeople use to illustrate their points in legislative sessions and television appearances alike.

On the other hand, the riddle lead can occasionally be used for more serious pieces as well. The columnist Peter Millar used the following lead for a piece on a potentially dangerous third party candidate who gave the two leading Austrian parties a bad scare in a 1994 election. The piece, which appeared in the international newspaper the *European*, was entitled "The mighty mouse who shook Austria."

> *What's the best way to ruin the sex life of two uncomfortably married elephants? Answer: put a sharp-toothed mouse in their bed. Welcome to the laugh-a-minute, deadly serious world of Austrian politics, where last weekend's election gave a huge boost*

to a party led by a smooth-talking radical in a trench coat who once posed half-naked for a women's magazine and, equally memorably, praised Adolf Hitler's employment policies.[16]

STATE YOUR CASE

When writing opinion pieces, the best lead is often the simplest—a strong statement of the argument you intend to make.

Singapore's government is to be applauded for refusing to reconsider Michael Peter Fay's sentence to six strokes of the cane for spray-painting cars there last September. Rather than condemn Singapore, we should consider following its lead.[17]

This lead leaves no question as to where the writer stands. The editorial piece that followed explained the pro-caning position in more detail, and made a direct, strong case for it.

MAKE A PREDICTION

Prediction is a dangerous thing for a journalist. As long as it is couched in terms such as "expected" or "might," however, it can be a useful way of introducing certain stories.

This kind of lead is most common in the "keeping the story alive" story. That is, a story dealing with an ongoing, long-term phenomenon that has sustained great public interest but has not made any breaking news. *USA Today*, for example, used the following lead in a story about the case of the ex–football star O. J. Simpson, who was about to be tried for murder in California. The story appeared four weeks into the pretrial skirmishing, on a Monday following a weekend in which there had been no fresh news about the case:

> *Judge Lance Ito is expected to rule as early as today whether he'll restrict—even throw out—key DNA test results in the O. J. Simpson murder case.*[18]

In this situation, the writers of the article must have hoped that the prospective, or predicted, event was enough to lure readers into a piece that turned out to be mostly a rehash of developments that took place the week before.

USE SOMEONE ELSE'S WORDS

A sharp or dramatic quote can make an ideal lead. A 1989 *Newsweek* article on a controversial foreign policy of the then president, George Bush, began with this attack by a Bush opponent:

> *At the very time freedom and democracy are receiving standing ovations in Europe, our president is sitting politely in the audience with little to say and even less to contribute.*[19]

The article that followed was actually quite favorable to the president's policies. The lead, however, made clear that the president's policies were controversial. At the same time, it probably hooked at least two groups of readers, by raising the ire of those supporting the president's policies, and by pleasing those opposed to them.

A quote from an actual participant in an event, or even an on-the-scene observer, can sometimes bring home its significance in a particularly forceful way.

Consider this lead from a *Time* magazine story on the bloody civil war in the African nation of Rwanda:

> *"There are no devils left in hell," the missionary said. "They are all in Rwanda."*

This quote summed up the horror of the war so well that it was not only a telling lead for the article, it was printed in large letters on the cover of the magazine. The fact that this melodramatic declaration was made by a missionary who had witnessed the carnage firsthand gave it a power and authority that no more objective description of the bloodletting would have carried.

Quotes don't need to be so dramatic to make effective leads, however. They don't need to be dramatic at all. A story in the real estate section of the *New York Times* began with this unsensational lead: "'It works for me,' says Richard Firestone. 'Lots of people say they envy me, but they wouldn't do what I do.'"[20]

This lead is far from dramatic, but it is effective nonetheless. It raises a question in the reader's mind. *What does this Richard Firestone do? What is it that "works" for him, and why wouldn't other people do it, too, if they envy him for doing it?* The answer, it turns out, is that he commutes by air to his job in Los Angeles and elsewhere from his home in the little town of Whitefish, Montana. The article goes on to explain how modern technology is enabling a number of highly paid professional people to make the attractive mountain valley community their home, while pursuing careers hundreds of miles away.

READ YOUR OWN STORY

The lead comes first in the story, but that doesn't mean it has to be written first. Sometimes the lead only becomes obvious in the process of writing the bulk of the story. As the French philosopher Blaise Pascal explained, "The last thing one knows when writing is what to put first." At times, the lead can be found buried within the story itself. A paragraph or incident that starts out somewhere in the body of the piece can often be moved to the front, making a perfect introduction to the whole.

It could be a description of a person, a place, or an incident that you originally put in the piece to add color. Even a simple fact you originally added merely to illustrate a point may turn out to be just the hook to grab the reader's attention and draw her or him to your subject.

EIGHT

SHAPING THE STORY

We refer to news *stories*, but we too often forget that we are, in fact, writing *stories*.

In essence, the job is a simple one. Find your lead, tell the story, and go home. But it is nowhere near as easy as that description makes it sound. Ideally, a news story should have at least some of the elements of any good story: reader interest, suspense, progression, a beginning, a middle, and an end.

And, most important of all, good writing.

No book is going to make you a good writer. But there are ideas and techniques that can help you learn to put a story together. Some of those ideas and techniques we've already discussed in the chapter on leads. Inviting the readers into your story, giving them real people to identify with, painting scenes, revealing events in a dramatic form, putting them in context—all these are effective journalistic techniques, wherever they are used in your story. Apt quotes and telling facts will color any kind of piece.

But the most important requirements for writing an effective news story are the same as the requirements for writing any other kind of story—knowing the story you have to tell, and telling it.

FIVE W'S AND ONE H

According to an old saying, all good news stories provide the same essential information. Who. What. Where. When. And why. The five Ws.

The following is a typical single-paragraph news story, one that might appear in almost any newspaper in the country. Four of the five pieces of information are finished within the very first sentence. The remainder of the story is devoted to the fifth:

> *Roger Tremplow, of 496 N. Sutton Pl. [who], surrendered to Riverton police [what] at the 4th precinct station house [where] at noon yesterday [when]. Tremplow, who had been the object of a citywide search, had been sought as a suspect in the recent wave of residential burglaries that has been plaguing the north side. Questioned by reporters on his way to a cell in city jail, Tremplow explained that he had turned himself in because he was tired of life on the run. "I've had enough of always looking over my shoulder," he declared. "I'd rather get it over with. I'll take my chances in the courts" [why].*

Where appropriate, an H and an S are sometimes added to the old formula. The H stands for How, and the S for Significance. Once you have covered all seven of those letters in a story, your job as a news writer will be fulfilled.

THE UPSIDE-DOWN PYRAMID

The basic nature of every news story was summed up by Carole Rich in her excellent book, *Writing and Reporting News: A Coaching Method:* "A news story is based on one main idea with supporting points."[1]

This does not mean that all news stories have exactly the same structure, of course. That "one main idea" can be expressed in many different ways. A variety of supporting points can be chosen, and arranged in any number of possible forms.

Despite this potential for diversity, the majority of all news stories do have the same basic shape or form. It is known as the inverted pyramid. The form is called that because, like a pyramid turned upside down, it is broadest at the top. That is, it begins with a summary lead, which gives the gist of the information contained in the story—the main idea. It then proceeds to flesh out the story, starting with the most important pieces of information, and descending down to the least important.

There are good reasons why the inverted pyramid is the most common of all news story forms. It is the single most helpful shape for both readers and editors. Readers like it because it gives them the heart of the story right away. This allows them to stop reading, if that is all they want to know, or to read on if they're interested in getting more detail. Editors like it because inverted pyramid stories are easy to cut. An editor who needs more space can just lop a paragraph or two off from the end, knowing that it is the least important information that is being cut.

THE PYRAMID, RIGHT SIDE UP

If the inverted pyramid is the most common shape for a news story, the second most common shape is the same pyramid turned right side up.

The pyramid story is a journalistic version of the classic short story form used by many fiction writers. It is a simple chronological telling of the story, with the climax—the key news—coming at or near the end.

The lead is especially important to a pyramid

story. It must suggest enough to pique the readers' interest, and entice them into reading on. Once they're hooked, the flow of the story itself must keep them reading through to the end.

The greatest advantage of the pyramid is also its greatest disadvantage: the reader doesn't know what is going to happen until the end. When the story is compelling enough, and the writing is good enough, this makes for suspense. When they are not, however, it makes for confusion, boredom, and disinterest.

The pyramid, then, is a more challenging form to write than the inverted pyramid. But it can be more rewarding, because it offers more opportunity to develop and display your narrative skills.

OTHER COMMON STORY FORMS

The pyramid and the inverted pyramid are the two most common story forms, but there are many others. In fact, there is no real limit to the number of forms a story may take except the writer's imagination and the editor's tolerance. Some forms, however, are more common than others. They can be described in different ways, and they are known by different names, but most veteran reporters use them more or less instinctively. Among them:

THE HOURGLASS • This is a combination of the two pyramid forms, with the pyramid on the bottom, and the inverted pyramid balanced on top.

Like the inverted pyramid, it begins with a summary lead containing the main idea, followed by a substantial amount of supporting information. This can be in the form of further details of the main event, or an explanation of the event's significance. This accomplished, the hourglass form starts over, in effect, shifting to a chronological retelling of the

120

entire story, preferably with an important fact or revelation coming at the end.

SECTIONS OR CHAPTERS • In this form, an overall lead is followed by a succession of separate sections, like the chapters of a book. Each is a kind of story in itself, with its own lead, and its own structure. But again, like the chapters of a book, each also relates to the others and furthers the progress of the story as a whole.

This form is only practical for long pieces, so it is usually reserved for feature stories, or for major investigative pieces. Depending on the nature of the story, the chapters can be arranged according to a variety of organizing principles. Each, for example, could be a chronological telling of one part of the story. Or each could present a different person's reactions to the same central event. An election story, for example, might be divided into sections, one giving the reactions of the winner, another of the loser, and the third of a knowledgeable political observer.

Similarly, an event could be examined from several different perspectives. A story about the passage of a controversial tax bill could have sections dealing with the actual provisions of the bill, the political maneuverings that got it passed, the economic impact of the new taxes, and the likely response of the voters at the next election.

THE LIST • This is the structure that is being used for this section of the current chapter. It consists of a lead, followed by an enumeration of several separate points, along with whatever explanation is necessary to make their significance clear. The list form can be used for whole stories, or for sections within a more elaborate story. It is particularly handy when you're dealing with a number of similar elements, such as key figures from a financial report; political candidates running for the same office; cheap vacation spots; a variety of bills passed by a legislature, or the separate provisions of a single bill.

BE CREATIVE

We have just discussed some of the traditional shapes of standard news stories. It is worthwhile to learn these journalistic conventions, and necessary to be able to use them. But you shouldn't be a slave to them. Not every story fits a standard mold. Some of the best stories are written from an unusual angle, or in an unusual form.

For example, in June 1994 Del Jones and James Cox of *USA Today* found a new way to do a piece on the effects of smoking. This was, of course, a familiar subject. The damage associated with smoking had been reported frequently since 1962, the year a landmark Surgeon General's report first declared smoking a major health hazard.

Familiar as it was, it was still an important story. Hundreds of thousands of Americans were still dying each year of tobacco-related diseases, and communities all over the country were passing laws to ban smoking in public places. But how were they to make this three-decade-old story new in 1994? To solve their problem, Jones and Cox took this old story and moved it ahead, beyond the present and into the future: "Say tobacco vanished from the USA today for reasons unknown. A court decision, perhaps. Or space aliens. Whatever the reason, it's gone. Poof!"[2]

After this provocative lead, they went on to describe how life would be different in this imaginary, tobacco-free future. By framing their story as a fantasy, they were able to give their readers some grim statistics with a cheery, humorous spin.

"[M]edical costs will fall substantially," they explained, "but only until the nation's 45 million ex-smokers come down with diseases of old age. In the meantime, they'll be hanging around draining . . . the Social Security System, when many used to die so cost-effectively at about 62." The multibillion-dollar tobacco industry would be wiped out, of course. "Livelihoods are being snuffed out. But the good news is that over the next ten years the 400,000 people who die each year from smoking will live an average seven to eight years longer—unless they start choking to death on gum, hard candy, toothpicks and celery sticks."[3]

THE KICKER

The end of a story—or kicker—may not be as important as the beginning, but it can help give shape and body to the whole. Robert J. Dvorchak, of the Associated Press, compares a kicker to a bootlace. "Unless you can tie a story together, it just won't fit right." He suggests ending with a strong quote, "or a snappy paragraph that serves as a knockout punch."

Besides rounding things off for the reader, a good kicker can discourage your editor from simply chopping off the end of your story. Dvorchak quotes Roy Peter Clark of the Poynter Institute for Media Studies, who says this about good news writers: "Their endings are so good that it is almost impossible to cut their stories from the bottom. They want their stories to be seamless or connected by a single thread. They want readers to read every word."[4]

NINE

QUESTIONS OF STYLE

Style is hard to define. It is made up of all the variable aspects of the writer's craft, everything that makes up your "voice" as a writer, and all the choices that go into writing your story.

Each writer has his or her own style. That is, each writer tends to make the same kinds of choices again and again, and those choices are different, to some extent, from the choices another writer would make. This is why, if five different writers wrote stories about the same event, each story would be different from each of the others.

Style is really determined by two different levels of choices. The first level is made up of the broad choices—questions of perspective, person, tone, length, and color—that have to be answered for every story you write. The second level is made up of those little choices of wording and punctuation that have to be answered for virtually every sentence.

THE BROAD QUESTIONS

Perspective

The first choice you must make when you sit down to write a story will be determined by the nature of your publication, the nature of the events you'll be writing about, and the perspective your readers will have toward those events. These issues will determine the perspective you should use in writing the story.

Ask yourself the following questions:

- Who are my readers?
- What is the significance of this event to *them*? Why should they—or why do they—care about it?
- What do they *need* to know about it? What do they *want* to know?

Say the local school board releases the budget for the coming school year, and you are assigned to write a story about it. The budget is a ten-page document, filled with figures. The bottom line is clearly important. What will the total budget be? But, beyond that, how should you report the story? Which figures should you emphasize? That depends on your readers and the nature of your publication.

If you are writing for a local daily newspaper, with a wide range of readers, you need to present a wide range of information. Besides reporting the bottom line, you need to break down the figures, and explain how the money will be allocated: what will be used for grade schools, for high schools; what will go toward teachers' salaries, or for custodians, for administrators; what will be spent on books or computers; this much for maintenance, this much for new construction. And so on—as much detail as you have room for in your piece.

In addition to the numbers, you may want to explore how these expenditures are likely to affect the schools, the students, and the community at large. Will it mean more teachers, or less? Will it lead to rising or lowering taxes? And so on.

If you are writing for a more specialized publication, with a more limited readership, you need to emphasize specific figures and specific effects. If you're writing for the West Side High School paper, for instance, you will report mostly on what the new budget will mean for your particular school. How much will West Side High get? How will the money be used? Will the library be expanded? Will extracurricular activities be cut?

If you're writing for a teachers' newsletter or magazine, on the other hand, your focus will be how the budget will affect teachers. Will salaries go up? Will new staff be hired, or will present teachers have to leave?

If you are writing for a publication aimed at parents, your main emphasis will be the budget's effect on the education of their children. If you are writing for a publication aimed at elderly people, who are too old to have children in school, your focus will be its effect on property taxes.

Your perspective may depend not only on the nature of publication where your story will appear, but also on the page on which it will appear. If you're writing for the sports page, for instance, you will write little or nothing about the budget's effect on education. Readers turn to the sports page for information about one thing, and one thing only: sports. This means your story will be about the new budget's effect on school sports. What will it mean for the high school football and basketball programs? Will girls' sports be increased? Will some sports have to be dropped?

To sum up: your story's perspective will be determined by a combination of two things: the nature of the event being reported, and the nature of your readership.

Person
Straight news stories are usually written in the third person. "Mayor Arnold B. Simpson officiated at the

opening of the new city hall. . . ." "The war in Bosnia heated up yesterday, when Serb troops resumed shelling. . . ." "Students at Madison Senior High protested the elimination of football from the school's athletic program. . . ."

The third person is appropriate to most news stories because the reporter has no place in them. He or she is reporting the doings of other people, or events that happened to others. What's more, the use of the third person helps to give the story a sense of objectivity.

But there are exceptions to this rule. The first person may be used in accounts of events the reporter witnessed firsthand. For example, a piece on the aftermath of a massacre in a Palestinian refugee camp in Lebanon began with this first-person account:

> They were everywhere, in the road, in laneways, in backyards and broken rooms, beneath crumpled masonry and across the top of garbage tips. The murderers—the Christian militiamen whom Israel had let in to "flush out the terrorists" fourteen hours before had only just left. In some cases the blood was still wet on the ground. When we had seen a hundred bodies, we stopped counting.[1]

In this case, use of the first person gives the reporter's account an authority it would lack without it.

Use of the first person can be desirable when the reporter has some special insight to share as a result of his or her direct experience. The first person may actually be required when a question of bias might arise as the result of a reporter's personal involvement in the events he or she is covering. A writer who was a participant in the event being reported ought to say so. A reporter for a college paper who took part in a campus demonstration that turned violent, for example, ought to mention her or his participation in any story written about the event.

This is true no matter how objective the reporter tries to be in writing the story. If they know the writer took part, readers may reasonably suspect that the writer's emotions enter into the way she or he saw and responded to the event. They have the right to know that the reporter was a participant.

Unlike most straight news stories, opinion pieces are often written in the first person. Such pieces are specifically meant as expressions of the writer's views, and so it is appropriate for the writer to speak in her or his own voice. "I find it shocking that . . ." "The older I get, the more it seems to me . . ." Sometimes, the first person can be used in a plural or collective voice: "As a nation, we've got to realize . . ."

The second person—speaking directly to the reader as "you" —should be used only rarely. It is too familiar for most kinds of newswriting. It implies a kind of personal relationship with the reader that a journalist is not expected to have. It can also have a lecturing, almost chiding, ring to it: as though the journalist were some kind of authority, setting the reader straight.

In general, you should be wary of using the second person in straight newswriting. It is rarely appropriate, except when asking readers a question, as you might do in a lead, or when inviting them to speculate.

The second person is ideally suited to certain kinds of journalism, however. It is particularly appropriate for how-to pieces, such as certain forms of travel writing, which involve giving instructions to the reader.

Color

According to an old saying, "The devil is in the details." Genius, someone once added, is in them, too. When it comes to writing news stories, details provide color and shading. A well-chosen detail can brighten your account, or darken it, cast a deep shadow, or shine an unexpected ray of light.

Police Sergeant Joe Friday of the old radio and television series *Dragnet* demanded one thing, and one thing only, from the witnesses he questioned: "Just the facts, ma'am."

Some journalists feel the same way. They think that all a news story really needs are the basic facts—the five Ws. Anything else is just filler. But any story can benefit from the addition of some appropriate color. Without color, in fact, any story is likely to be dull.

The term "color" refers to the details that flesh out the bare skeleton of a story. A telling quote. A description of the clothes a murder victim was wearing when she was stabbed. The breed of the dog the suspect was walking when the police picked him up. The slogans on the signs of protestors at a political rally. The stutter in the voice of the little boy as he thanked the lifeguard who rescued him from the undertow.

The amount and nature of the color you include in your story will depend, to a great extent, on all the other questions we've already dealt with. The key to the use of color is to make the details you include express the meaning you have found in the story, and communicate that meaning to your readers.

Length

Any event, no matter how simple or complex, can be reported at almost any length. The length of your story will depend on a number of things, including the amount of detail you use, how much background you include, and the extent to which you use color.

What length is best for a particular story? That depends on the newsworthiness of the event being reported—and more specifically, on the event's newsworthiness *for your publication*. The same event will be, and should be, reported at different lengths in different publications.

The following examples demonstrate how the same local story might be told at three different lengths. The first is no more than a brief item:

> *Riverville police today announced the arrest of Alden Kasitch, 28, for the murder of his wife, Sandy, 25. Her body was found Friday morning, in the backyard of the couple's home at 3225 Garland Avenue. Kasitch is expected to be arraigned this afternoon.*

The second adds more detail:

> *After a week-long investigation, Riverville police arrested 28-year-old Alden Kasitch this morning for the murder of his 25-year-old-wife, Sandy. Police say that suspicion had centered on the husband almost from the beginning of their investigation into the death of the attractive young high school teacher, whose body Kasitch claimed to have found in the couple's backyard at 3225 Garland Avenue when he was leaving for work last Friday morning. An autopsy revealed that she had been beaten to death.*

> *Questioned by police and the press, Kasitch has denied any connection with his wife's death. He claims that his wife had left*

their home Thursday evening for an unknown destination, and that he neither saw nor heard from her until he discovered her body Friday morning as he was leaving for work.

Kasitch looked calm and resigned arriving at police headquarters this morning. He is expected to be arraigned this afternoon.

The third adds more color, and puts the particular event being reported in a broader social context:

When 28-year-old Alden Kasitch was called from his place on the assembly line at Ritter Engine in Riverville this morning, he found two policemen waiting for him. One of them read him his rights as they placed him under arrest for the murder of his wife, Sandy, 25.

The arrest was not unexpected. Police attention had centered on her husband from the moment the badly beaten body of the attractive blond schoolteacher was found in the backyard of her home at 3225 Garland Avenue last Friday morning. Neighbors reported frequent loud arguments coming from the Kasitch home, arguments that often ended with violent sounds, indicating the smashing of furniture. Mrs. Kasitch's fellow teachers at Conklin High School told police that she had twice come to work with facial bruises, and once with a black eye. Alden Kasitch's fellow workers at Ritter Engine acknowledged that he had a terrible temper, and had once physically assaulted a co-worker in a dispute over a can of soda.

For the past week, police investigators and forensic teams have combed over the Kasitch house and backyard, as well as the family automobile. They have refused to comment on the evidence they have collected, but they clearly feel that it is sufficient to make an arrest.

If the police are right, the Kasitch killing fits into the syndrome of domestic violence that has become an increasing social concern in recent years. Highly publicized cases, many involving celebrities such as O. J. Simpson and Mickey Rourke, along with several studies revealing the prevalence of domestic violence, have focused public attention on the problem of spousal abuse, and particularly of violence by husbands against their wives.

Police say that one out of every two women murdered in the United States is killed by her husband, or someone else with whom they are intimate. According to Ann Jones, author of Next Time She'll be Dead: Battering and How to Stop It, battering is the most often committed crime in the United States, and more than one million American women are treated for the resulting injuries each year.

Questioned by police and the press, however, Kasitch has steadfastly denied any connection with his wife's death. He claims that his wife left their home Thursday evening for an unknown destination, and that he had not seen or heard from her until he discovered her body Friday morning as he was leaving for work.

Kasitch is a thin young man with dark hair and a bushy mustache. Belying reports of his violent temper, police report that he has been consistently soft-spoken and polite in conversation with them, as he has when speaking to *reporters. Arriving at police headquarters around 10:30 this morning, he seemed calm and resigned as he was led in handcuffs from the police car into the station. Detective Sergeant Raymond Carter, who participated in the arrest, later said that the suspect seemed "awfully cool" for someone being arrested for murder.*

Jason Freeman, the local attorney Kasitch has hired to defend him, reasserted his client's claim of innocence this afternoon at an impromptu news conference at City Hall. Kasitch, he said, is doing "as well as can expected under the terrible circumstances," and dismissed Kasitch's apparent coolness by explaining that his client felt "almost relieved" that the weeklong "ordeal of uncertainty he has suffered through has at least been resolved."

Kasitch is scheduled to be arraigned at 5:30 this afternoon.

The first, very brief item, would be appropriate if Riverville were a large city, in which domestic murders were relatively commonplace, and not ordinarily considered major news events. Similarly, such a short item would be suitable for a local Riverville "shopper" or other specialized publication that reported, but did not emphasize, crime news. Or in a paper published in a city some distance away from Riverville, which did not circulate there.

The second might appear in a local daily if Riverville were a middle-sized city, in which the case would be of moderate local interest. The third might appear in a publication which, either because of the size of the community or the nature of the case, considered the Kasitch murder a major news story.

Most often, of course, the question of length will not be determined by you but by your editor. Your story will be as long as your editor has space to give it.

THE "LITTLE QUESTIONS"

Some editors will leave the little questions of word choice and punctuation up to the writer, but many will not. Unfortunately, individual writing style is not as valued in modern newsrooms as it once was. Some editors, in fact, do everything they can to stamp it out, insisting that all writers follow common rules for everything from punctuation to the length of sentences.

For the most part, these rules are arbitrary. Many publications insist that their writers put a final comma before the "and" that concludes a list, or series. For example: "The barnyard was filled with a motley assortment of cows, horses, dogs, and chickens." The Associated Press, however, rejects this so-called serial comma. If the barnyard was being described by AP, it would contain "a motley assortment of cows, horses, dogs and chickens."

Your publication may have its own style guide, which sets down strict rules for such questions. If so, you will need to follow them. Even if you are lucky enough to write for a publication that allows great freedom of style, however, there are certain style tips on which most news writers and editors would agree:

Shorter Is Better

Long-windedness may be appropriate in certain forms of writing, but not in journalism. If a sentence, a paragraph, or a whole news story is long, it should be because it needs to contain a lot of information, not because it is written in a wordy manner.

The Fewer Letters the Better

What's true of sentences is also true of words. Don't use long ones where short ones will do. With rare exceptions, "magic" is better than "prestidigitation," "hard" is better than "laborious," "trip" is better than "excursion," and "a bit" is better than "a modicum."

Simplify Your Tenses

In general, use the simplest tense available. In most cases this turns out to be either the present tense or the simple past. Compound tenses are usually unnecessarily complicated. They tend to slow down your sentences and distract the reader. Used too much, they create a kind of mental maze which readers have to struggle to solve.

There Is/It Is

Start as few sentences as possible with "there is," "there are," or "it is." *There* is nothing inherently wrong with these forms. *It is* just that they easily become repetitious and therefore boring. *There is* really no need for them most of the time, and yet, *there is* a tendency for writers to use them as crutches. *It is* common for writers to fall into the habit of using them too much, and *it is* also often the case that sentences and clauses that are introduced by them become unnecessarily long, complex, and clumsy. *It is* annoying when this is the result of their use.

Don't Be Afraid to Punctuate

Some writers shy away from colons and semicolons. They think they're too "fancy" or pretentious. In reality, such devices can help make your sentences move along more smoothly and rapidly.

Rewrite

Unless driven to the wall by a relentless deadline and a merciless editor, never turn in the first draft of a story. At least one rewrite is absolutely necessary, and more would be even better. No story, and very few sentences, come out right the first time. What's more, the longer the time you can allow between the first writing and the rewrite, the better the final story is likely to be.

One good way to tell if your story has the flow and clarity of good writing is to read it aloud to yourself. If it doesn't sound right to you, it won't read right to your readers, either. Whenever you find yourself stumbling over a clumsy phrase, or getting tongue-tied in the middle of a jumbled sentence, you need to make some changes.

Focus on Meaning

Both in writing and rewriting, focus on the meaning of what you write and the style will take care of itself. If you can't decide how to say something, chances are that you're not sure what you want to say. Keep asking yourself: What do I really mean here? What is the key point I'm trying to get across?

Don't Be a Slave to Rules—Not Even These Rules

The only absolute requirements of good newswriting are to be accurate, clear, and readable. The final goal is not to be grammatically or stylistically correct, it is to communicate with the reader. If any rule gets in the way of doing this, break it.

$\mathcal{S}$URCE NOTES

CHAPTER 1

1. Commission on Freedom of the Press, *A Free and Responsible Press* (Chicago: University of Chicago Press, 1947).

CHAPTER 2

1. The Missouri Group, *News Reporting & Writing* (New York: St. Martin's Press, 1992), p. 150.

CHAPTER 5

1. *Ethics in America*, The Annenberg CPB Project, as cablecast over Mind Extension University, July 18, 1994.

2. The A.S.N.E. Statement of Principles is available from the American Society of Newspaper Editors. It can also be found in its entirety in Bruce M. Swain's *Reporter's Ethics* (Ames: Iowa State University Press, 1978).

3. Speaking at the Forum on the Clinton Agenda and Congress, sponsored by Lazlo & Associates, and cablecast live on C-SPAN, Sept. 7, 1994.

4. Personal conversation, Sept 6, 1986.

5. The U.S. Supreme Court decision in the case of *Kimmerle* v. *New York,* N.Y. 262 N.Y. 99 (1933) 502.

6. *New York Times Co.* v. *Sullivan* 376 U.S. 254 (1964), 8.

CHAPTER 6

1. Quoted in Michael Kronenwetter's *Journalism Ethics* (New York: Franklin Watts, 1988), p. 97.

2. "Journalists Roundtable," C-SPAN, July 15, 1994.

3. Speaking at a conference on investigative reporting, sponsored by the Regional Reporters Association, Washington, D.C., September 9, 1994, and televised on C-SPAN.

4. Perhaps the best study of this phenomenon is *The People and the Press*, a Times Mirror Investigation of Public Attitudes Toward the News Media, conducted for Times Mirror by the Gallup Organization in 1986.

CHAPTER 7

1. Herman Melville, *Moby Dick*; or *The White Whale* (New York: Dodd, Mead and Company), p. 1.

2. Rafael Sabatini, *Scaramouche* (New York: Houghton Mifflin, 1921), p. 1.

3. William A. Welch, "Haitians Cut Deal to Quit," *USA Today*, Sept. 19, 1994.

4. Robert Young, "LBJ: WON'T RUN," *Chicago Tribune*, on April 1, 1968.

5. Karen Brandon, "Illegal immigration: A drain or an asset?" *Chicago Tribune*, Oct. 18, 1994.

6. Bill Keller, "A Deadly Feud Tears at Enclave on Gorbachev's Southern Flank," as published in *The*

Collapse of Communism edited by Bernard Gwertzman and Michael T. Kaufman (New York: Times Books/Random House, 1990), 145-151. First published in *The New York Times*.

7. Bruce W. Nelan, "Days of Trauma and Fear," *Time*, April 4, 1994, p. 33.

8. Jo Sandin, "State's schools become battlegrounds," *The Milwaukee Journal*, April 17, 1994.

9. Paul Shrivastava, "Picture It: Burger Boxes Outlasting the Pyramids," *Los Angeles Times*, May 18, 1990.

10. Richard Benedetto, "Doubts dog president's every move, every poll," *USA Today*, June 9, 1994.

11. Kelly C. Thayer, "Insurance may not cover landfill cleanup," *Wausau Daily Herald*, June 18, 1994.

12. Kelly C. Thayer, "Altered States," *Wausau Daily Herald*, June 26, 1994.

13. Eugene Linden, "Population: The Awkward Truth," *Time*, June 20, 1994, p. 74.

14. Gabriel Constans, "Suu Kyi's Message," *The Atlanta Journal/The Atlanta Constitution*, March 20, 1993.

15. Elaine S. Povich, "Newest Growth Industry on Capitol Hill: Charts," *Chicago Tribune*, August 25, 1994.

16. Peter Millar, "The mighty mouse who shook Austria," *The European*, October 14–20, 1994.

17. Heather Stern Little, "Bring back the birch," (editorial), *USA Today*, April 5, 1994.

18. Gale Holland and Sally Ann Stewart, "Simpson case enters Week 4," *USA Today*, Oct. 17, 1994.

19. Russell Watson, and others, "No Time for Showboating," *Newsweek*, November 27, 1989, p. 30.

20. Ellin Bard, "Commuter Homes Rise in Montana Valley," *The New York Times*, June 19, 1994.

CHAPTER 8

1. Carole Rich. *Writing and Reporting News: A Coaching Method* (Belmont, Calif.: Wadsworth, 1994), p. 5.

2. Del Jones and James Cox, "What would our lives be like?" *USA Today*, June 9, 1994.

3. *Ibid.*

4. Robert J. Dvorchak, letter to Lydia Stein of Franklin Watts, November 11, 1994.

CHAPTER 9

1. Robert Fisk, *The Times* (London), September 20, 1982; reprinted in *Eyewitness to History*, edited by John Carey (New York: Avon, 1987), pp. 679-683.

BIBLIOGRAPHY

Brady, John. *The Craft of Interviewing.* Cincinnati: Writer's Digest, 1976.

Cappon, Rene J. *Associated Press Guide to News Writing.* New York: Prentice Hall, 1991.

Commission on Freedom of the Press. *A Free and Responsible Press.* Chicago: University of Chicago Press, 1947.

Goldstein, Tom. *The News at Any Cost.* New York: Simon & Schuster, 1985.

Kronenwetter, Michael. *Journalism Ethics.* New York: Franklin Watts, 1988.

Lanson, Gerald, and Mitchell Stephens. *Writing & Reporting the News.* Fort Worth: Harcourt Brace College Publishers, 1994.

Merrill, John C., and Ralph D. Barney, eds. Ethics and the Press: *Readings in Mass Media Morality.* New York: Macmillan, 1975.

Missouri Group, The: Brian S. Brooks, George Kennedy, Daryl R. Moen and Don Ranly. *News Reporting & Writing.* 4th edition. New York: St. Martin's Press, 1992.

Rich, Carole. *Writing and Reporting News: A Coaching Method.* Belmont, Calif.: Wadsworth Publishing Press, 1994.

Ruehlmann, William. *Stalking the Feature Story.* Cincinnati: Writer's Digest, 1977.

Swain, Bruce M. *Reporter's Ethics.* Ames: Iowa State University Press, 1978.

INDEX